I0447021

Congressional Research Service

Environmental Regulation and Agriculture

Megan Stubbs, Coordinator
Analyst in Agricultural Conservation and Natural Resources Policy

June 20, 2012

Congressional Research Service
7-5700
www.crs.gov
R41622

CRS Report for Congress
Prepared for Members and Committees of Congress

Summary

As the U.S. and global economies continue to struggle, some inside and outside of Congress have expressed concern about how environmental regulation may stifle growth and productivity. Much of the criticism has focused on environmental regulations promulgated by the Environmental Protection Agency (EPA). Some claim that EPA is overreaching its regulatory authority and imposing costly and burdensome requirements on society. The agriculture community, among others, has been vocal in its concerns, contending that EPA appears to be focusing some of its recent regulatory efforts on agriculture. Environmental advocates, on the other hand, support many of EPA's overall regulatory efforts to protect public health and the environment. Where agriculture contributes to environmental impairment, these groups say, it is appropriate to consider ways to minimize or eliminate the adverse impacts.

A healthy agriculture industry and a healthy environment are both important to the nation. However, agricultural production can have varying impacts on the environment. The use of both natural resources and synthetic inputs in agricultural production can sometimes create a negative impact on human health and the surrounding ecosystem. The magnitude of these environmental impacts varies widely across the country and changes over time. Given the agricultural sector's size and potential to affect its surrounding environment, there is interest in tightening environmental policies while also maintaining an economically viable industry. Most recognize the agriculture community's efforts to protect natural resources while striving to maintain a sustainable and abundant food supply.

The current federal response to environmental issues associated with agriculture is viewed as being both restrictive and supportive. Traditionally, farm and ranch operations have been exempt or excluded from many environmental regulations. The challenges and complexity of regulating numerous crop and livestock operations can be cost-prohibitive for government regulators; thus environmental policies have historically focused on large industrial sources such as factories and power plants, not farms. Much of the current farm policy addressing environmental concerns is through economic incentives to encourage beneficial production practices.

Growing interest in the impact of EPA's regulatory actions on many sectors of the economy is evident in Congress, which has been examining the roles of EPA and other federal agencies in regulating environmental protection. Among the broad options for Congress, besides conducting general oversight, are reviewing rules under the Congressional Review Act, amending current law to modify an agency's authority, introducing freestanding legislation, or using appropriations bills to prevent funds from being used for specific actions.

The majority of environmental regulations that could affect agriculture are administered by EPA, though not all. In some cases, agriculture is the direct or primary focus of the regulatory actions. In other cases, agriculture is one of many affected sectors. Of particular interest to agriculture are regulatory actions affecting air, water, energy, and chemicals. Issues associated with air (e.g., dust and emissions) and water quality (e.g., fertilizer and nutrient run-off) are a primary focus of many regulations affecting agriculture because of agriculture's potential to affect these resources. Changes in energy policy, namely bioenergy, have recently become important to many in the agricultural industry based on the potential of corn-based biofuel production to contribute to the nation's energy supply. The risks associated with agricultural chemical use and possible impacts on human health and the environment have also led to recent federal regulatory reviews of chemical fertilizer and pesticide use.

Contents

Figures

Tables

Contacts

Introduction

A healthy agriculture industry and a healthy environment are both important to the nation. However, agricultural production can have varying impacts on the environment. The use of both natural resources (e.g., soil and water) and synthetic inputs (e.g., fertilizers and pesticides) in agricultural production can sometimes create a negative impact on the surrounding ecosystem. For example, soil erosion, farm chemical runoff, and overgrazing can affect water and air resources. Converting grassland prairies and wetlands to crop production can impact wildlife populations. The magnitude of these environmental impacts varies widely across the country and changes over time.

The federal response to agriculture's impact on the environment can be viewed at opposite ends of a spectrum: incentivizing sustainable production (carrot) versus requiring it through regulation (stick). While most within the agriculture community prefer the "carrot" approach, there is an increasing focus on the "stick" because of recent federal regulatory action. Current federal environmental policies both restrict and encourage certain production practices. The ultimate mix of policy instruments depends on the nature of the resource issue and the information available on the linkages between farming activities and the environmental resources.

Traditionally, farm and ranch operations have been exempt or excluded from many federal environmental statutes and regulations. Attempting to regulate numerous individual crop and livestock operations can be cost-prohibitive for government regulators, and environmental policies have historically focused on large industrial sources such as factories and power plants. Therefore, much of the current federal farm policy addressing environmental concerns is in large part voluntary; that is, it seeks to encourage agriculture producers to adopt conservation practices through economic incentives. Most environmental regulation, in terms of permitting, inspection, and enforcement, is done by state and local governments, typically based on regulatory guidance issued by the U.S. Environmental Protection Agency (EPA). Many point out that the relative number of environmental regulations affecting agriculture is small compared to other industries. However, given the agricultural sector's size in the landscape[1] and its potential to affect its surrounding environment, there is interest in both tightening environmental policies and also maintaining an economically viable agriculture industry.

The EPA is the primary federal authority for administering environmental protection polices, while the U.S. Department of Agriculture (USDA) is the primary federal authority for incentivizing agricultural production. USDA provides both educational outreach and technical and financial assistance opportunities for producers to implement environmentally sustainable practices.[2] While many of these voluntary programs and policies have been in place for decades and have had considerable success, some question whether a strictly voluntary approach to agricultural conservation generates enough environmental gains.[3] EPA, on the other hand, has

---

[1] A total of 1.9 billion acres of land and water cover the contiguous 48 states, of which 71% is non-federal rural land (nearly 1.4 billion acres). Non-federal rural lands are predominantly rangeland (409 million acres), forest land (406 million acres), and cropland (357 million acres). Source: USDA, NRCS, *2007 National Resources Inventory*, Summary Report, Washington, DC, December 2009, p. 6, http://www.nrcs.usda.gov/technical/NRI/2007/2007_NRI_Summary.pdf.

[2] For more information, see CRS Report R40763, *Agricultural Conservation A Guide to Programs*.

[3] Michelle Perez, Craig Cox, and Ken Cook, *Facing Facts in the Chesapeake Bay*, Environmental Working Group, September 2009, http://www.ewg.org/files/chesapeake-bay-pollution.pdf.

recently received criticism from some lawmakers and industry leaders for appearing to focus some of its recent regulatory efforts on agriculture.[4] Some claim EPA has overreached its regulatory authority.[5] The agriculture community, among others, has been vocal in its displeasure with recent EPA regulatory proposals and the costs associated with protecting public health and the environment.[6]

These criticisms are reflected in recent legislative proposals that restrict or prohibit certain regulatory actions.[7] Beyond the criticism of individual regulations, there also are calls for broad regulatory reforms, for example, to reinforce the role of economic considerations in agency decision making or to increase Congress's role in approving or disapproving regulatory decisions. Congress will likely continue to give attention to EPA's and other federal agencies' roles in regulating environmental protection. Both the Senate and House Committees on Agriculture have shown particular interest in EPA's actions and conducted oversight hearings on regulatory impacts to agriculture during the 112th Congress.[8]

Report Content and Caveats

This report covers select federal environmental regulations that could affect agriculture.[9] The report is intended to provide the background, status, and issues related to environmental regulations or initiatives possibly affecting agriculture. Many of these issues are commonly referred to as being of concern to agriculture based on media and industry reports. Their inclusion in this report is not intended to suggest or imply that the regulation or action has either a beneficial or harmful effect on agriculture or to what degree. Similarly, regulatory actions not included in this report do not indicate the lack of potential impact on the agriculture sector.

This report only addresses federal regulatory actions. In many cases, constraints on agricultural production to reduce pollution emissions arise at the state level in response to local concerns. State and local regulations are not specifically included in this report, but may be discussed generally where appropriate. Actions considered voluntary or in response to regulatory actions are also not included. This means that many USDA programs and initiatives, which offer funding to

---

[4] Examples of congressional press releases and letters regarding EPA may be found here: Rep. Frank Lucas - http://www.house.gov/htbin/blog_inc?BLOG,ok03_lucas,blog,999,All,Item%20not%20found,ID= 100305_3660,TEMPLATE=postingdetail.shtml; Rep. Collin Peterson - http://collinpeterson.house.gov/press/111th/ Peterson%20calls%20for%20bipartisan%20action%20against%20the%20EPA.html; Sen. Inhofe and Sen. Snowe - http://epw.senate.gov/public/index.cfm?FuseAction=Minority.Blogs; and Sen. Chambliss and Sen. Roberts - http://chambliss.senate.gov/public/index.cfm?p=PressReleases&ContentRecord_id=f7607094-43ca-45c6-a789-3f91e18e1cca&ContentType_id=5c81ba67-be20-4229-a615-966ecb0ccad6&Group_id=29a81778-8944-46e0-a550-9d034534e70a.

[5] The Wall Street Journal, "The EPA Permitorium," editorial, November 22, 2010.

[6] American Farm Bureau, "EPA's Regulatory Diet is Unhealthy for America," press release, February 2011, http://fb.org/index.php?fuseaction=newsroom.agenda.

[7] For example, the House-passed long-term continuing resolution H.R. 1, which is discussed further below. For more information, see CRS Report R41698, *H.R. 1 Full-Year FY2011 Continuing Resolution Overview of Environmental Protection Agency (EPA) Provisions*.

[8] For example, U.S. Congress, Senate Committee on Agriculture, Nutrition, and Forestry, *Oversight Hearing to Examine the Impact of EPA Regulation on Agriculture*, 111th Cong., 2nd sess., September 23, 2010; and U.S. Congress, House Committee on Agriculture, *Public Hearing to Review the Impact of EPA Regulation on Agriculture*, 112th Cong., 1st sess., March 10, 2011.

[9] For additional information regarding EPA regulations beyond those affecting agriculture, see CRS Report R41561, *EPA Regulations Too Much, Too Little, or On Track?*.

---

agricultural producers to preclude the need for environmental regulation, are not discussed in this report.

The majority of the regulations discussed in this report are administered by EPA, though not all. In some cases, agriculture is the direct or primary focus of the regulatory actions. In other cases, agriculture is one of many affected sectors. In many cases, for a regulation to become effective, EPA rules must be adopted by states to which the program has been delegated (e.g., most environmental permitting programs are delegated to qualified states). Moreover, many states require that the state legislature review new regulations before the new rules would take effect. The general regulatory development and compliance process can be tedious and complex. In some cases, the promulgation and implementation of regulations may take years.[10] In the case of some environmental regulations, the agencies must adhere to court-ordered deadlines.[11]

General Options for Congress

Most congressional committees conduct oversight hearings on agency activities and programs throughout the legislative session. Given the interest in the issues described in this report, it is likely that oversight hearings will continue in the 112th Congress. If Congress decides to explore the way federal agencies regulate environmental issues, there are at least four sets of options available.

One option is the Congressional Review Act (CRA).[12] The CRA establishes special congressional procedures for disapproving a broad range of regulatory rules issued by federal agencies. Before any rule covered by CRA can take effect, the federal agency that promulgates the rule must submit it to Congress. If Congress passes a joint resolution disapproving the rule under procedures provided by the act, and the resolution becomes law, the rule cannot take effect or continue in effect. Also, the agency may not reissue either that rule or any substantially similar one, except under authority of a subsequently enacted law. The path to enactment of such a resolution could be a steep one and still subject to presidential veto. Overriding a veto requires a two-thirds majority in both the House and Senate.[13]

Another, more comprehensive option would be to amend current law to modify the regulating agency's authority. Bills using this approach in connection with some environmental regulatory issues were introduced in the 111th Congress but were not enacted.[14] While this might be the preferred option by some, including the Administration, the challenges associated with crafting the specifics of a bill acceptable to a majority could remain difficult.[15] From an agricultural

---

[10] Some regulations do not become effective immediately. In some cases, the regulation takes effect over time or gradually expands to affect more individuals. Virtually all major EPA regulatory actions are subjected to court challenge, which also delays the implementation.

[11] Court-ordered dates for proposed or promulgated regulations may change. It is not uncommon for EPA to request extensions of time, often due to the need to analyze extensive comments.

[12] 5 U.S.C. §§801-808.

[13] For additional information on the Congressional Review Act, see CRS Report RL31160, *Disapproval of Regulations by Congress Procedure Under the Congressional Review Act*.

[14] For example, the House passed H.R. 2454, and the Senate Environment and Public Works Committee reported S. 1733. These bills would have amended the Clean Air Act (CAA) to establish an economy-wide cap-and-trade program for greenhouse gases (GHGs) and HFCs, preserved EPA's authority to regulate GHG emissions, and required new standards for uncapped major sources of GHGs, among other things.

[15] For example, amending the CAA to revoke some existing regulatory authority as it pertains to GHGs while (continued...)

perspective, this option may be even more challenging. While committees may exert certain oversight powers, there are jurisdictional issues to be considered.[16] In many cases environmental laws with potential to affect agriculture originate outside of the House and Senate Agriculture Committees. Although the issues associated with agriculture could still be of interest within other committees, it might not be a central focus. On the other hand, agricultural interests in Congress have achieved some previous success on cross-jurisdictional issues.[17]

To provide a more detailed response to the issue than what might be permitted under the CRA, a third option would be to introduce freestanding legislation. By specifically identifying issues and prescribing regulatory direction, stand-alone legislation may address many of the issues with the current regulatory approach but still face challenges similar to those of amending existing law. While freestanding legislation could also amend existing law, this option may be designed to be more acceptable to Members willing to consider a delay of regulatory action, as opposed to overturning or blocking regulatory action altogether.[18] In effect, freestanding legislation could buy time for additional action to be taken by Congress.

Another option that Congress could consider is to include an amendment on the agency's appropriations bill that prevents funds from being used for specific actions. This was done in the FY2010 Interior, Environment, and Related Agencies Appropriations Act,[19] in which provisions restricted or prohibited the use of EPA funds for certain climate change regulatory activities affecting livestock operations. Because neither the House nor the Senate Appropriations Committees reported FY2011 EPA appropriations in the 111th Congress, these provisions from FY2010 appropriations were carried forward and the restricting provisions remained in effect under the multiple continuing resolutions (CRs). Additional restrictions were present in H.R. 1, the House-passed full-year CR for FY2011. As passed by the House, the bill included specific funding levels for a number of EPA accounts and activities. It also contained more than 20 provisions restricting or prohibiting the use of appropriated funds to implement various regulatory activities under the EPA's jurisdiction—including many discussed in this report. On March 9, 2011, the Senate failed to approve House-passed H.R. 1 and subsequently also did not agree to a substitute text (S.Amdt. 149) that contained different funding levels and generally omitted the EPA regulatory provisions in the House-passed bill.[20] In reporting H.R. 2584, which would have provided EPA funding for FY2012, the House Appropriations Committee included more than 25

(...continued)

establishing new authority designed specifically to address their emissions is the approach advocated by the Administration and, indeed, by many participants in the climate debate regardless of their position on EPA's regulatory initiatives. For additional discussion, see CRS Report R41212, *EPA Regulation of Greenhouse Gases Congressional Responses and Options*.

[16] For additional information on committee jurisdiction, see CRS Report 98-175, *House Committee Jurisdiction and Referral Rules and Practice* and CRS Report 98-242, *Committee Jurisdiction and Referral in the Senate*.

[17] For example, in the 111th Congress a Manager's Amendment to major climate change legislation added a full title specifically directed toward agriculture. Title V of H.R. 2454, created an offset program for agriculture and forestry related practices to be run by USDA, rather than EPA.

[18] An example of freestanding legislation proposed in the 112th Congress is H.R. 910 and its Senate counter part, S. 482. These bills known as the Energy Tax Prevention Act of 2011, would restrict EPA authority and repeal a dozen EPA regulatory actions dealing with GHGs. The House Energy and Commerce Committee approved H.R. 910 and the Senate counterpart (S. 482) was debated as an amendment to S. 493 during the week of March 14, 2011.

[19] P.L. 111-88, for additional information, see CRS Report R41149, *Environmental Protection Agency (EPA) Appropriations for FY2011*.

[20] For information, see CRS Report R41698, *H.R. 1 Full-Year FY2011 Continuing Resolution Overview of Environmental Protection Agency (EPA) Provisions*.

---

provisions intended to restrict or preclude the use of funds to proceed with recent or pending EPA regulatory actions.[21] These provisions were not included in the final appropriation (P.L. 112-74, enacted in December 2011).[22]

Report Organization

The remainder of this report is organized under four broad subheadings: Air, Water, Energy, and Chemicals. Each section includes selected regulatory actions and provides background information and statutory authority, followed by the current status of the rule or regulatory action and issues identified or raised by the agricultural community regarding the regulatory action. Finally, each section identifies the appropriate CRS specialist for additional information; these contacts are also listed in **Table 1**.

Table 1. CRS Specialists on Environmental Issues

Issue Area	CRS Specialist	Contact Information
Clean Water Act	Claudia Copeland	ccopeland@crs.loc.gov, 7-7227
Endangered Species Act	Lynne Corn	lcorn@crs.loc.gov, 7-7267
Clean Air Act, particulate matter	Rob Esworthy	resworthy@crs.loc.gov, 7-7236
Clean Air Act	Jim McCarthy	jmccarthy@crs.loc.gov, 7-7225
Spill prevention	Jonathan Ramseur	jramseur@crs.loc.gov, 7-7919
Toxic Substances Control Act, pesticides	Linda-Jo Schierow	lschierow@crs.loc.gov, 7-7279
Agriculture-based biofuels, ethanol	Randy Schnepf	rschnepf@crs.loc.gov, 7-4277
Voluntary agriculture conservation	Megan Stubbs	mstubbs@crs.loc.gov, 7-8707
Clean Air Act, mobile sources, biofuels	Brent Yacobucci	byacobucci@crs.loc.gov, 7-9662

Air

Agricultural production practices from both livestock and crop operations generate a variety of substances that enter the atmosphere, potentially creating health and environmental issues. Agriculture's effect on air quality rose to national importance in the 1930s, when the conversion of native grasslands to cropland caused severe dust storms known as the Dust Bowl. The federal response to this phenomenon created many of the conservation outreach and education programs that remain in place today.[23] While dust storms of this proportion are rare in the United States today, issues associated with soil erosion, particulates and farm chemical emissions, and livestock odor are still of concern.

The following section covers five federal regulations relating to air, including:

- mandatory reporting of greenhouse gases (GHGs);

---

[21] For information, see CRS Report R41979, *Environmental Protection Agency (EPA) FY2012 Appropriations Overview of Provisions in H.R. 2584 as Reported.*

[22] CRS Report R42332, *Environmental Protection Agency (EPA) FY2012 Appropriations.*

[23] For additional information, see CRS Report RL34069, *Technical Assistance for Agriculture Conservation.*

- GHG emissions tailoring rule and the "cow tax";

- reductions of emissions from gasoline/diesel powered stationary engines;

- national ambient air quality standards (particulate matter and ozone); and

- Emergency Planning and Community Right-to-Know Act (EPCRA) and Comprehensive Environmental Response, Compensation, and Liability Act (CERCLA) reporting requirements.

Mandatory Reporting of Greenhouse Gases (GHGs)

EPA was required by the FY2008 Consolidated Appropriations Act[24] "to develop and publish a ... final rule not later than 18 months after the date of enactment of this Act, to require mandatory reporting of greenhouse gas (GHG) emissions above appropriate thresholds in all sectors of the economy of the United States."

On October 30, 2009, EPA promulgated the final Greenhouse Gas Reporting Rule.[25] The rule requires suppliers of fossil fuels or industrial gases, manufacturers of vehicles and engines, owners or operators of electric power plants, and other—mostly industrial—sources to report their emissions of GHGs to EPA annually, beginning in 2011. Covered entities are required to report to EPA if they emit 25,000 tons or more of carbon dioxide or the equivalent amount of five other GHGs (methane, nitrous oxide, hydrofluorocarbons, perfluorocarbons, and sulfur hexafluoride and other fluorinated gases). About 10,000 facilities in 31 categories of sources were covered by the rule, as promulgated. EPA subsequently added 11 other categories of sources.

Status

The only agricultural sources covered by the Reporting Rule are manure management systems that emit methane and nitrous oxide in amounts greater than the reporting threshold. EPA identified six specific categories of agricultural sources that could be subject to the rule: beef cattle feedlots; dairy cattle and milk production facilities; hog and pig farms; chicken egg production facilities; turkey production; and broilers and other meat type chicken production. In all, EPA estimates that 107 livestock facilities nationwide would need to report under the rule.

In EPA's FY2010 appropriations act,[26] however, Congress included language barring EPA from using funds under that act to implement mandatory GHG reporting by manure management facilities. This prohibition was carried over into FY2011 and FY2012 by the continuing resolutions that funded EPA's continued operation and by the Consolidated Appropriations Act for FY2012, P.L. 112-74. Therefore, despite the inclusion of manure management systems among the regulated entities, no agricultural sources are currently required to comply with the Reporting Rule.

---

[24] P.L. 110-161.

[25] U.S. Environmental Protection Agency, "Mandatory Reporting of Greenhouse Gases," 74 *Federal Register* 56260, October 30, 2009.

[26] Department of the Interior, Environment, and Related Agencies Appropriations Act, 2010, P.L. 111-88.

Issues

For the facilities required to report, the rule imposes little cost because it only requires monitoring and reporting, and the monitoring does not require direct measurement of emissions. EPA considered requiring direct measurement of GHG emissions from manure management systems, but rejected the approach due to what it termed "the extreme expense and complexity of such a measurement program."[27] Instead, the agency promulgated an approach that allows the use of default factors, such as a system emission factor, for certain elements of the calculation, combined with the use of site-specific data (e.g., number of livestock). EPA estimated the total annual cost of the rule for the 107 potentially affected manure management facilities at $300,000.

In comments on the proposed rule, a number of agricultural stakeholders noted that agriculture as a whole is responsible for less than 1% of total GHGs emitted and questioned why manure management systems in particular were included in the proposal. Other categories of agricultural sources, such as livestock enteric fermentation and soil management, emit larger amounts of methane and nitrous oxide. EPA explained that it did not include reporting by the other agriculture categories because, for those sources, no direct GHG emission measurement methods are available except for expensive and complex equipment. Using emissions estimates for such sources, instead of direct measurement, would have a high degree of uncertainty and could burden a large number of small emitters.

Commenters also expressed concern about the difficulty that livestock facilities might have in determining whether or not they are subject to the rule. In response, EPA modified the proposal to remove manure sampling requirements and instead will allow facilities to use default values for estimating emissions. The threshold table within the final rule (**Table 2**) identifies animal population threshold levels below which facilities are not required to report emissions.

Table 2. EPA Animal Population Threshold Below Which Facilities Are Not Required to Report GHG Emissions

Animal Group	Average Animal Population (Head)
Beef	29,300
Dairy	3,200
Swine	34,100
Poultry:	
Layers	723,600
Broilers	38,160,000
Turkeys	7,710,000

Source: U.S. Environmental Protection Agency, "Mandatory Reporting of Greenhouse Gases," 74 *Federal Register* 56485, October 30, 2009.

Notes: For all animal groups except dairy, the average annual animal population represents the total number of animals present at the facility. For dairy facilities, the average annual animal population represents the number of mature dairy cows present at the facility. For additional information, see Table JJ-1 of the Environmental Protection Agency, "Mandatory Reporting of Greenhouse Gases," 74 *Federal Register* 56485, October 30, 2009.

---

[27] U.S. Environmental Protection Agency, "Mandatory Reporting of Greenhouse Gases," 74 *Federal Register* 56339, October 30, 2009.

CRS Contacts

Claudia Copeland, Specialist in Resources and Environmental Policy, 7-7227, ccopeland@crs.loc.gov, or Jim McCarthy, Specialist in Environmental Policy, 7-7225, jmccarthy@crs.loc.gov.

GHG Emissions Tailoring Rule and the "Cow Tax"

EPA promulgated standards for GHG emissions from new light duty motor vehicles on May 7, 2010 (see "Motor Vehicle and Heavy-Duty Truck GHG Rule and Corporate Average Fuel Economy (CAFE) Standards," below).[28] The standards themselves are not considered particularly controversial, but their implementation, on January 2, 2011, triggered two other requirements of the Clean Air Act (CAA) that apply to stationary sources. The first of these is a requirement that stationary sources emitting any air pollutant "subject to regulation" under the act must obtain a permit under Title V of the CAA (Title V permit) if they emit more than 100 tons per year of the pollutant subject to regulation. Agricultural sources, such as confined animal feeding operations (CAFOs), are among those that could potentially be subject to this permit requirement. Because permit applicants must pay a fee to cover the costs of administering the permit program, many in the agriculture community have referred to this requirement as the "cow tax."

The second requirement triggered by implementation of the motor vehicle standards is a requirement that new or modified stationary sources emitting more than 100 or 250 tons annually of any pollutant subject to regulation under the act must obtain pre-construction permits (referred to as "PSD" permits) and install Best Available Control Technology (BACT) to reduce emissions.

Status

On June 3, 2010, EPA promulgated a rule that sets higher thresholds for the Title V permit and PSD/BACT requirements that would apply to GHG emissions.[29] EPA says that under the promulgated rule, the agency has not identified any agricultural sources that would be required to obtain permits for GHG emissions, and therefore none would be subject to BACT requirements.[30]

Under the rule, called the GHG "Tailoring Rule," the threshold initially is annual emissions of 75,000 tons of carbon dioxide equivalents, not 100 or 250 tons as required for other pollutants by the PSD and Title V permits. With this threshold, the nation's largest GHG emitters, including power plants, refineries, cement production facilities and about two dozen other categories of

---

[28] U.S. Environmental Protection Agency, U.S. Department of Transportation, "Light-Duty Vehicle Greenhouse Gas Emission Standards and Corporate Average Fuel Economy Standards; Final Rule," 75 *Federal Register* 25324-25728, May 7, 2010.

[29] U.S. Environmental Protection Agency, "Prevention of Significant Deterioration and Title V Greenhouse Gas Tailoring Rule; Final Rule," 75 *Federal Register* 31514, June 3, 2010.

[30] EPA Briefing on the Tailoring Rule, House Energy and Commerce Committee, May 14, 2010. This issue is also discussed in RTI International, for U.S. EPA, "Regulatory Impact Analysis for the Final Prevention of Significant Deterioration and Title V Greenhouse Gas Tailoring Rule," Final Report, May 2010, pp. 64-66, at http://www.epa.gov/ttn/ecas/regdata/RIAs/riatailoring.pdf. A key reason that agricultural sources would not require permits is that EPA excludes what are called "fugitive emissions" from the emissions used to determine whether an agricultural source is a major source subject to permit requirements. Fugitive emissions are emissions that are not released through a stack or vent, or could not be reasonably collected and released through a stack or vent.

sources (an estimated 17,000 facilities in all, or nearly 70% of the nation's largest stationary source GHG emitters) are the only sources required to obtain permits. Farms, smaller businesses, and large residential structures (about 6 million sources in all these categories), which would otherwise be required to obtain permits after GHGs became subject to regulation, are shielded from permitting requirements, including permit fees.

The June 2010 Tailoring Rule does not permanently exempt smaller sources. In promulgating the rule, EPA said it expected to lower the threshold, but not below 50,000 tons of GHG emissions, through separate rule-making that would take effect in 2013. The agency has subsequently decided not to lower the threshold and has also stated that, within five years of the rule's promulgation, EPA and state permitting authorities would conduct a study of the permitting authorities' ability to administer more inclusive PSD and Title V permit programs. Within a year of the study's completion, EPA and state permitting authorities would conduct rulemaking for this phase of the program. The study might confirm the threshold, revise it, or establish other streamlining techniques for subsequent permitting activity. It is unclear how agricultural sources might be affected by these potential rule changes.

In the FY2010 appropriations act for EPA,[31] Congress included a provision prohibiting EPA from using funds under the act to promulgate or implement any rule requiring the issuance of CAA Title V permits for GHG emissions associated with livestock production. This prohibition was carried over into FY2011 and FY2012 by the subsequent appropriations measures that have funded EPA's continued operation.

Issues

The issues related to the Tailoring Rule are similar to those raised by the "Mandatory Reporting of Greenhouse Gases (GHGs)," discussed above. The rule itself appears to exempt all agricultural sources by its high thresholds and the exclusion of fugitive emissions, but many are concerned about whether EPA intends to consider any agricultural sources as subject to regulation under future Clean Air Act GHG rules.

CRS Contacts

Claudia Copeland, Specialist in Resources and Environmental Policy, 7-7227, ccopeland@crs.loc.gov, or Jim McCarthy, Specialist in Environmental Policy, 7-7225, jmccarthy@crs.loc.gov.

Reduction of Emissions from Gasoline/Diesel Powered Stationary Engines

On June 15, 2004, EPA promulgated emission control standards for hazardous air pollutants emitted by gasoline- and diesel-powered stationary engines. This is primarily of concern to agricultural operations that rely on gas and diesel engines for irrigation pumping. The standards are generally referred to as the RICE (Reciprocating Internal Combustion Engine) rules. Besides setting emission standards, the rules would have exempted these engines from emission controls

---

[31] P.L. 111-88.

during startup, shutdown, and periods of malfunction. On December 18, 2008, the D.C. Circuit Court of Appeals ruled that the standards must address emissions during all phases of operation, including periods of startup, shutdown, and malfunction. As a result, the court vacated and remanded the rules to EPA.

Status

EPA subsequently divided the standards into two regulatory actions. On March 3, 2010, it issued a final rule for existing diesel-powered stationary engines.[32] The rule will apply to more than 900,000 stationary engines used as generators and to power pumps in industrial and agricultural settings. EPA issued final emissions standards for existing stationary engines that burn gasoline, natural gas, and landfill gas, known as spark ignition engines, on August 20, 2010.[33]

Issues

The proposed rules were criticized by some state permitting authorities and industry groups as being unworkable, difficult to enforce, and perhaps unnecessary in rural settings. In response to these comments, EPA stated that most engines used by agricultural sources are smaller than 300 horsepower, and will be subject only to required management practices (e.g., frequency of oil changes). Catalysts or other control equipment would not be required.

CRS Contact

Jim McCarthy, Specialist in Environmental Policy, 7-7225, jmccarthy@crs.loc.gov.

National Ambient Air Quality Standards (NAAQS)— Particulate Matter

National Ambient Air Quality Standards (NAAQS) are standards for outdoor (ambient) air that are intended to protect public health and welfare from harmful concentrations of pollution. NAAQS are at the core of the Clean Air Act, even though they do not directly regulate emissions. In essence, they are standards that define what EPA considers to be clean air. Once a NAAQS has been set, the agency, using monitoring data and other information submitted by the states, identifies areas that exceed the standard and must, therefore, reduce pollutant concentrations to achieve it. After these "nonattainment" areas are identified, state and local governments have up to three years to produce State Implementation Plans that outline the measures they will implement to reduce the pollution levels and attain the standards.

NAAQS have been set for six pollutants. The two that affect the largest number of areas are those for ozone and particulate matter (PM). Because some farming and livestock practices contribute to particulate matter emissions and because particulate matter and ozone can affect agricultural

---

[32] U.S. Environmental Protection Agency, "National Emission Standards for Hazardous Air Pollutants: Reciprocating Internal Combustion Engines; Final Rule," 75 *Federal Register* 9648, March 3, 2010.

[33] U.S. Environmental Protection Agency, "National Emission Standards for Hazardous Air Pollutants for Reciprocating Internal Combustion Engines; Final Rule," 75 *Federal Register* 51570, August 20, 2010.

productivity, the agricultural community continues to show particular interest in these standards. NAAQS ozone issues are discussed in the next section.

Status

As ordered by the U.S. District Circuit Court for the District of Columbia,[34] EPA released its proposed revisions to the current PM NAAQS on June 15, 2012. The proposal includes options for potentially tightening certain aspects of the "fine" particulate matter or $PM_{2.5}$ (particles less than or equal to 2.5 micrometers (μm) in diameter) standards, but not for still inhalable particles less than or equal to 10 micrometers (PM_{10}), referred to as thoracic coarse particles.[35] As part of its agreement submitted to the court, EPA agreed to issue final revised PM NAAQS by December 2012. This current EPA periodic review of the PM standards as mandated by statute[36] was initiated as implementation of the current 2006 PM NAAQS continues.

EPA promulgated its previous final revisions to the PM NAAQS and the associated national air quality monitoring requirements on October 17, 2006,[37] primarily strengthening the preexisting (1997) $PM_{2.5}$. The 2006 PM NAAQS revisions did not strengthen the existing annual standard for PM_{10}.[38] Several states and industry, agriculture, business, and environmental and public health advocacy groups petitioned the U.S. Court of Appeals for the District of Columbia Circuit, challenging certain aspects of EPA's 2006 revisions. A February 24, 2009, decision by the D.C. Circuit granted the petitions, in part, while denying other challenges. The court did not vacate the PM standards but remanded certain aspects of the annual $PM_{2.5}$ NAAQS standard to EPA for reconsideration.[39]

The 2006 revised NAAQS, which are now being implemented, primarily affect urban areas: 120 counties and portions of counties in 18 states have been designated nonattainment areas for $PM_{2.5}$ by EPA based on 2006-2008 air quality monitoring data. Final designations for the 2006 PM NAAQS were published November 13, 2009. The majority of the roughly 3,000 counties throughout the United States (including tribal lands) were designated attainment/unclassifiable, and are not required to impose additional emission control measures to reduce $PM_{2.5}$. For those 120 counties designated nonattainment for $PM_{2.5}$, states have until November 2012 to submit state

---

[34] *American Lung Ass'n v. EPA*, D D.C., No. 1:12-cv-243, order issued 6/6/12.

[35] See EPA's Fact Sheet and other related documents regarding the June 15, 2012 proposal at http://www.epa.gov/pm/actions.html#jun12.

[36] Section 109(d)(1) of the Clean Air Act requires EPA to review the NAAQS and the scientific information upon which they are based at five-year intervals.

[37] U.S. Environmental Protection Agency, "National Ambient Air Quality Standards for Particulate Matter," 71 *Federal Register* 61144-61233, October 17, 2006; and U.S. Environmental Protection Agency, "Revisions to Ambient Air Monitoring Regulations," 71 *Federal Register* 61236-61238, October 17, 2006. EPA indicated that it would be expanding its research and monitoring programs to collect additional evidence on the differences between thoracic coarse particles typically found in urban areas and those typically found in rural areas. Some stakeholders have expressed concern about EPA's monitoring efforts in rural areas and the future implications monitoring results could have for those areas. Currently, EPA has stated that its monitoring efforts to measure PM are primarily research-driven for the purpose of establishing necessary scientific criteria, and not for enforcement purposes.

[38] For additional information, see CRS Report RL34762, *The National Ambient Air Quality Standards (NAAQS) for Particulate Matter (PM) EPA's 2006 Revisions and Associated Issues*, by Robert Esworthy and James E. McCarthy.

[39] The court remanded the primary annual $PM_{2.5}$ standard and the secondary $PM_{2.5}$ standards to EPA. The court upheld EPA's decision to retain the 24-hour PM_{10} standard to provide protection from thoracic coarse particle exposures and to revoke the annual PM_{10} standard (*American Farm Bureau Federation v. U.S. EPA*, No. 06-1410, D.C. Cir., February 24, 2009).

implementation plans (SIPs) identifying specific regulations and emission control requirements that would bring an area into compliance with the standard.[40]

The EPA did not designate any new nonattainment areas for PM_{10} NAAQS since the standards were not strengthened by the 2006 NAAQS revision. To the contrary, a number of counties previously designated nonattainment have been determined by EPA to be in attainment since the 2006 NAAQS revisions. As indicated in **Figure 1**, below, the majority of the counties throughout the United States (including tribal lands) are designated attainment/unclassifiable for the PM_{10} NAAQS. As of March 30, 2012, 42 of the original 87 areas designated nonattainment for PM_{10} in 1991 had been redesignated to maintenance.[41] As shown in **Figure 1**, the remaining 45 areas are either meeting the PM_{10} NAAQS based on 2008-2011 data and awaiting consideration for redesignation, have incomplete data, or remain nonattainment.[42] Those areas previously designated nonattainment for the PM_{10} NAAQS typically include, or were adjacent to, densely populated localities, where PM monitors are frequently located. Only a subset of PM_{10} NAAQS nonattainment areas in California and Arizona have SIPs that include requirements related to agricultural operations in addition to requirements for other sources.

---

[40] For additional information, see CRS Report R40096, *2006 National Ambient Air Quality Standards (NAAQS) for Fine Particulate Matter (PM2.5) Designating Nonattainment Areas*, by Robert Esworthy.

[41] See EPA's PM_{10} designations at http://www.epa.gov/air/oaqps/greenbk/pindex.html.

[42] According to information provided to CRS by EPA's Office of Air Quality Planning and Standards (OAQPS) on April 23, 2012, 13 areas are meeting the PM_{10} NAAQS based on 2008-2010 air quality data. States have submitted maintenance plans for 5 of these 13, and EPA has published clean data determinations for an additional 2 (of the 13) areas to suspend the PM_{10} attainment plan requirement. Additionally, 19 areas have incomplete data and 13 areas remain nonattainment based on 2008-2010 air quality data.

Figure 1. Status of PM₁₀ Nonattainment Areas

(based on 2008-2010 air quality; many areas are only portions of counties)

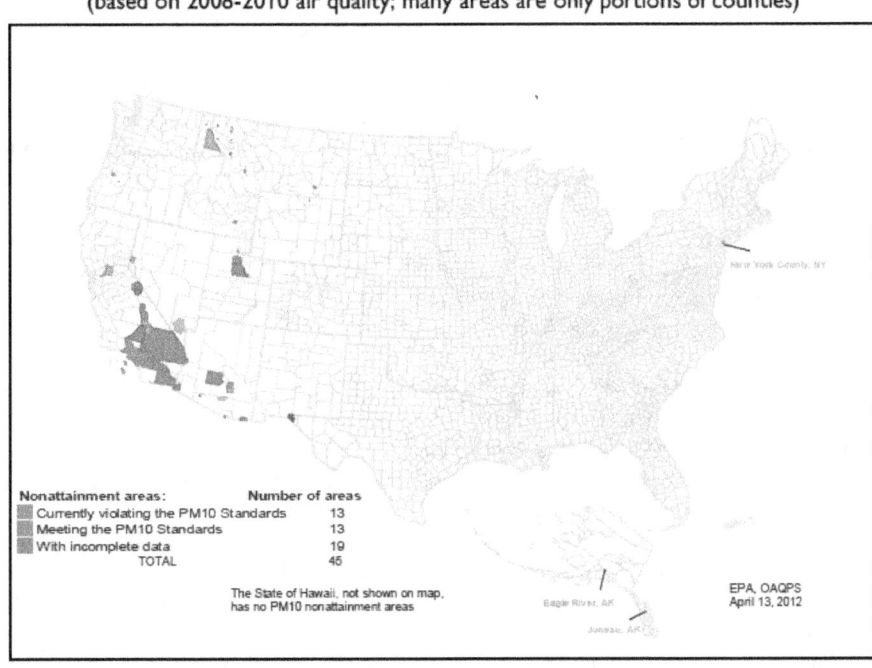

Source: Provided to CRS by the EPA Office of Air Quality Planning and Standards, April 13, 2012.

Notes: Areas not highlighted on the map are designated attainment/unclassifiable. There are no PM₁₀ nonattainment areas in Hawaii, which was not included on the EPA map. For more information, see CRS Report RL34762, *The National Ambient Air Quality Standards (NAAQS) for Particulate Matter (PM): EPA's 2006 Revisions and Associated Issues.*

Issues

The agricultural community has generally been more concerned with EPA's review and potential changes of the PM₁₀ NAAQS than with the PM₂.₅ NAAQS.[43] Thoracic coarse particles (PM₁₀) are generally emitted as a result of mechanical processes that crush or grind larger particles or the resuspension of dusts.[44] While certain agricultural operations can contribute to emission of PM₁₀—sometimes referred to as "farm dust"—there are many sources of thoracic coarse particles, for example, unpaved and paved roads, traffic-related emissions such as tire and brake lining materials, direct emissions from industrial operations, construction and demolition activities, and mining operations. EPA has noted that atmospheric science and monitoring information indicates that exposures to PM₁₀ tend to be higher in urban areas than in nearby rural locations.[45] Urban or industrial ambient mixes of PM₁₀ dominated by high-density vehicular, industrial, and

---

[43] There was some concern regarding designations in rural areas for the 2006 PM₂.₅ NAAQS. The designated nonattainment areas for the PM₂.₅ are primarily concentrated in and around highly populated metropolitan areas.

[44] U.S. Environmental Protection Agency, "National Ambient Air Quality Standards for Particulate Matter," 71 *Federal Register* 61146, October 17, 2006.

[45] U.S. Environmental Protection Agency, "Review of the National Ambient Air Quality Standards for Particulate Matter: Policy Assessment of Scientific and Technical Information," p. 2-36, OAQPS Staff Paper EPA-452/R-05-005a, December 2005, http://www.epa.gov/ttn/naaqs/standards/pm/data/pmstaffpaper_20051221.pdf.

construction emissions have been the primary concern with respect to reducing the negative health effects. EPA continues to research the link between coarse particle composition and toxicity, including the toxicity of urban versus rural particles.

On April 22, 2011, EPA released a final staff policy assessment as part of its ongoing PM NAAQS review.[46] This assessment, which addresses both fine ($PM_{2.5}$) and coarse (PM_{10}) particulates, summarized EPA staff conclusions regarding the broadest range of policy options based on available scientific evidence, air quality assessments, and analyses. With regard to PM_{10}, EPA staff concluded that it would be appropriate to consider either retaining or revising the current 24-hour (daily) PM_{10} standard, depending on the weight placed on the evidence and its associated uncertainties and limitations. The Clean Air Scientific Advisory Committee (CASAC) did not initially support retaining the current primary PM_{10} standard and recommended consideration of revising the standard in order to increase public health protection.[47]

In letters to the EPA Administrator[48] and during oversight hearings,[49] some Members of Congress raised concerns about EPA's staff draft reports, CASAC recommendations, and the potential impacts that tightening the PM_{10} NAAQS standards could have on the agricultural industry. Many Members encouraged EPA to retain the current PM_{10} NAAQS standards. In response to these concerns, and those raised by stakeholders in the agricultural community, EPA released a fact sheet summarizing the PM_{10} NAAQS standards in the context of agricultural activities[50] and held six public outreach or "listening" sessions in various regions of the country to discuss the PM NAAQS with an emphasis on the PM_{10} standards.[51] Subsequently, in October 14, 2011, letters to members of the Senate Committee on Agriculture, Nutrition, and Forestry, the EPA Administrator announced her intention to retain the current PM_{10} NAAQS standard with no revision.[52] Other Members urged the Administrator to include retaining the $PM_{2.5}$ as an option for consideration in

---

[46] U.S. Environmental Protection Agency, "Release of Final Document Related to the Review of the National Ambient Air Quality Standards for Particulate Matter," 76 *Federal Register* 22665, April 22, 2011, http://www.epa.gov/ttn/naaqs/standards/pm/data/20110419pmpafinal.pdf.

[47] Letter from Dr. Jonathan M. Samet, Chair, Clean Air Scientific Advisory Committee, to the Honorable Lisa P. Jackson, EPA Administrator. CASAC Review of *Policy Assessment for the Review of the PM NAAQS—Second External Review Draft*, 2010. Available at http://yosemite.epa.gov/sab/sabproduct nsf/264cb1227d55e02c85257402007446a4/CCF9F4C0500C500F8525779D0073C593/$File/EPA-CASAC-10-015-unsigned.pdf.

[48] Examples of letters to EPA Administrator Lisa Jackson include, but are not limited to, a joint letter from 21 Senators, July 23, 2010, http://grassley.senate.gov/about/upload/Agriculture-07-23-10-dust-letter-to-EPA-signed-version-doc.pdf; a joint letter from Senators Kent Conrad and Byron Dorgan and Representative Earl Pomeroy, August 5, 2010, http://conrad.senate.gov/pressroom/record.cfm?id=327070&; a joint letter from 75 House Members, September 27, 2010, http://agriculture.house.gov/pdf/letters/EPA_NAAQS.pdf; and a joint letter from 99 House Members, March 29, 2011, http://fincher.house.gov/press-release/fincher-noem-call-epa-abandon-unreasonable-dust-standards.

[49] See examples in footnote 8.

[50] "The U.S. Environmental Protection Agency's Coarse Particulate Matter PM_{10} Standards and Agriculture Fact Sheet," February 17, 2011, http://www.epa.gov/oar/oaqps/particlepollution/agriculture.html.

[51] Based on a June 9, 2011, presentation at the USDA NRCS Agricultural Air Quality Task Force Meeting, EPA summarized the following dates and locations for its outreach meetings: Washington, D.C. – February 17, 2011; Kansas City, MO (EPA Regions 6 & 7 states) – February 23, 2011; Des Moines, IA (EPA Regions 5 & 7 states) – February 25, 2011; Riverside, CA (EPA Region 9 states) – March 2, 2011; Spokane, WA (EPA Region 10 states); Denver, CO (EPA Region 8 states) - March 10, 2011, http://www.nrcs.usda.gov/Internet/FSE_DOCUMENTS/stelprdb1043120.pdf.

[52] Letter from Lisa Jackson, EPA Administrator, to Senator Debbie Stabenow and Senator Amy Klobuchar, October 14, 2011, http://www.epa.gov/air/particlepollution/actions.html.

---

the agency's proposal rule.[53] The EPA proposal for revising the PM NAAQS released June 15, 2012, would retain the existing PM_{10} standards, but proposed two options for strengthening certain aspects of the $PM_{2.5}$ standards and also proposed modifications to the associated monitoring network.[54]

Despite the EPA's proposal to retain the PM_{10}, some stakeholders remain skeptical that the final revised NAAQS could be changed from the proposal. Congress continues to consider legislation that would delay EPA regulatory action with respect to revising the PM_{10} NAAQS,[55] including the House-passed Farm Dust Regulation Prevention Act of 2011 (H.R. 1633), which awaits action in the Senate. A general provision was also included in FY2012 House-reported EPA appropriations language (H.R. 2584, Title IV, Sec. 454)[56] that would have restricted the use of FY2012 appropriations "to modify the national primary ambient air quality standard or the national secondary ambient air quality standard applicable to coarse particulate matter (generally referred to as "PM_{10}")."[57] No comparable provision was retained in the Consolidated Appropriations Act, 2012 (P.L. 112-74), enacted December 23, 2011, which ultimately included EPA's FY2012 appropriation.

CRS Contact

Robert Esworthy, Specialist in Environmental Policy, 7-7236, resworthy@crs.loc.gov.

National Ambient Air Quality Standards (NAAQS)—Ozone[58]

Under the CAA, EPA is to review the science for each of the NAAQS every five years, and either reaffirm or revise the standard. The EPA Administrator completed a review of the ozone NAAQS in March 2008, and made both the primary (health-based) and secondary (welfare-based) standards more stringent, but he did not set the standards within the ranges recommended by the independent panel of scientists that advises him (i.e., CASAC). He also rejected their advice to change the form of the secondary standard to better measure whether ozone concentrations were above levels needed to protect crops and forests from damage.[59] Challenged in court, EPA agreed to reconsider the March 2008 decisions (court decisions are discussed further below).

---

[53] See joint letter from Representatives Fred Upton, Chairman, Committee on Energy and Commerce, Ed Whitfield, Chairman, Subcommittee on Energy and Power, and Joe Barton, Chairman Emeritus, June 6, 2010, http://republicans.energycommerce.house.gov/Media/file/Letters/112th/060612EPANAAQS.pdf.

[54] See footnote 35.

[55] For example, U.S. Congress, House Committee on Energy and Commerce, Subcommittee on Energy and Power, *Farm Dust Regulation Prevention Act of 2011*, hearing on H.R. 1633, 112th Cong., 1st sess., October 25, 2011, http://energycommerce.house.gov/hearings/hearingdetail.aspx?NewsID=8999.

[56] The Department of the Interior, Environment, and Related Agencies Appropriations Act, 2012 (H.R. 2584, Title IV sec. 454) as reported by the House Committee on Appropriations on July 19, 2011. From July 25, 2011, to July 28, 2011, the House considered H.R. 2584 as reported July 19, 2011, but the House floor debate was suspended.

[57] See CRS Report R42332, *Environmental Protection Agency (EPA) FY2012 Appropriations*, by Robert Esworthy, and CRS Report R41979, *Environmental Protection Agency (EPA) FY2012 Appropriations Overview of Provisions in H.R. 2584 as Reported*, by Robert Esworthy.

[58] For additional background on NAAQS, see the previously discussed "National Ambient Air Quality Standards (NAAQS)—Particulate Matter" section.

[59] The damage that crops and vegetation suffer from ozone exposure is cumulative over the growing season. In order to better measure and provide protection against these impacts, EPA staff recommended a new seasonal (3-month) (continued...)

Status

On January 19, 2010, EPA proposed to strengthen the primary ozone NAAQS and to revise the form of the secondary standard as the agency's scientific advisers had recommended. Under the proposed revisions, the vast majority of counties with ozone monitors would be found in nonattainment of the primary standard, using the most recent available data, and many might violate the secondary standard, as well.

EPA expected to promulgate a final version in late summer 2011, but on September 2, 2011, the President requested that the agency withdraw its decision without promulgating it. Instead, the agency will continue a review that it aims to complete by 2014. EPA is also proposing new monitoring requirements for the states, with more monitors to be placed in rural areas.[60]

Issues

EPA will resume implementation of its 2008 ozone NAAQS, which affect few agricultural areas. Despite the withdrawal of what would have been an even more stringent standard, air quality is likely to improve as a result of regulations currently being phased in for cars, trucks, and electric power plants, among other sources.

Ultimately, the 2014 ozone NAAQS revision could be one of the more significant regulations promulgated by EPA, and could call attention to air quality problems in agricultural areas to a far greater extent than previous standards.

CRS Contact

Jim McCarthy, Specialist in Environmental Policy, 7-7225, jmccarthy@crs.loc.gov.

EPCRA and CERCLA Reporting Requirements

The Emergency Planning and Community Right-to-Know Act (EPCRA) and the Comprehensive Environmental Response, Compensation, and Liability Act (CERCLA, or Superfund) have reporting requirements that are triggered when specified quantities of certain substances are released to the environment, including ammonia and hydrogen sulfide. Both ammonia and hydrogen sulfide are chemicals generated by livestock manure, particularly swine and poultry, when in concentrated animal populations. Both CERCLA and EPCRA include citizen suit provisions that have been successfully used to take legal action against poultry and swine operations for violations of the reporting requirements of the laws. In 2005, a group of poultry producers petitioned EPA for an exemption from EPCRA and CERCLA release reporting requirements, arguing that releases from poultry growing operations pose little or no risk to

---

(...continued)

average for the secondary standard that would cumulate hourly ozone exposures for the daily 12-hour daylight window. Previously, the secondary standard simply measured the highest individual readings for any 8-hour period. CASAC agreed with this recommendation.

[60] For additional information on the proposed standards, see CRS Report R41062, *Ozone Air Quality Standards EPA's Proposed Revisions.*

public health, while reporting imposes an undue burden on producers and government responders.[61]

Status

In December 2008, EPA promulgated an EPCRA/CERCLA administrative reporting exemption for air releases.[62] The final rule exempts hazardous substance releases that are emitted to the air from all livestock operations (not just poultry farms) from CERCLA's requirement to report releases to the air to federal officials. It provides a partial exemption for such releases from EPCRA's requirement to report releases to state and local emergency officials: the final rule continues to apply EPCRA's reporting requirement to large CAFOs (those subject to Clean Water Act permitting, discussed below in the section on "Implementation of Existing Clean Water Act Permit Requirements for CAFOs"), but it exempts smaller facilities. The reporting exemptions in the final rule took effect January 20, 2009.

The 2008 rule was challenged by industry groups, including the National Pork Producers Council, as well as environmental advocates. Industry argued that CAFOs should be exempted from all reporting under Superfund and EPCRA because air emissions from animal feeding operations pose no threat to public health or the environment. Environmentalists also went to court, arguing that CAFOs should report under both laws because air emissions from animal feedings operations do pose a public health and environmental risk. The legal challenges were consolidated in the U.S. Court of Appeals for the District of Columbia (*Waterkeeper Alliance v. EPA*, D.C. Cir., No. 09-1017). In June 2010 the government asked the court to remand the 2008 rule for reconsideration and possible modification. The court approved the government's request in October 2010. EPA anticipates proposing a new or revised rule by August 2012. In the meantime, the rule remains in effect. According to press reports, EPA does not plan to directly regulate air emissions from animal feeding operations, but is seeking to require their reporting. Legislation has been introduced in the 112th Congress to exclude "manure" from the definition of hazardous substance under CERCLA and to remove reporting liability under CERCLA and EPCRA (H.R. 2997 and S. 1729).

Issues

The agriculture industry remains concerned about the potential burden on large CAFOs of complying with the EPCRA reporting requirements, even though the final rule exempted facilities that are not subject to Clean Water Act permitting (see "Implementation of Existing Clean Water Act Permit Requirements for CAFOs," below). Critics of the 2008 rule, including environmentalists and some state air quality officials, contend that the CERCLA and EPCRA reports provide good information about emissions that enable citizens to hold companies accountable in terms of how toxic chemicals are managed. Similarly, the agriculture industry is concerned about potential liability that could arise for animal operations if manure were to be defined as a "hazardous substance."

---

[61] For additional information, see CRS Report RL33691, *Animal Waste and Hazardous Substances Current Laws and Legislative Issues*.

[62] U.S. Environmental Protection Agency, "CERCLA/EPCRA Administrative Reporting Exemption for Air Releases," 73 *Federal Register* 76948-76960, December 18, 2008.

CRS Contact

Claudia Copeland, Specialist in Resources and Environmental Policy, 7-7227, ccopeland@crs.loc.gov.

Water

The release of sediment, nutrients, pathogens, and pesticides from agricultural production can degrade the quality of water resources. While it is widely believed that agriculture can have a significant impact on water quality, there is no comprehensive national study of agriculture's effect on water quality.[63] Several water quality assessments document degradation from agriculture practices; however, the extent and magnitude is difficult to measure because of its nonpoint nature.[64] Federal environmental laws, such as the Clean Water Act (CWA), largely do not regulate agricultural actors, in many cases giving the regulatory responsibilities to the states. Constraints on agricultural production to reduce pollution discharges typically arise at the state level in response to local concerns.[65]

The following section covers four regulations relating to water, including:

- implementation of existing Clean Water Act permit requirements for CAFOs;

- Chesapeake Bay protection and restoration;

- Florida nutrient water quality standards; and

- spill prevention control and countermeasure (SPCC) plans.

Implementation of Existing Clean Water Act Permit Requirements for CAFOs

Under the CWA, while most of agriculture is exempt from federal regulation, large CAFOs are defined as point sources and thus are subject to the act's prohibition against discharging pollutants into U.S. waters without a permit. In October 2008, EPA issued a regulation to revise a 2003 CWA rule governing waste discharges from CAFOs. This action was necessitated by a 2005 federal court decision (*Waterkeeper Alliance et al. v. EPA*, 399 F.3d 486 (2nd Cir. 2005)), resulting from challenges brought by agriculture industry groups and environmental advocacy groups that

---

[63] Marc Ribaudo and Robert Johansson, *Agricultural Resources and Environmental Indicators, 2006 Edition*, USDA, ERS, Economic Information Bulletin No. (EIB-16), Washington, DC, July 2006, p. 2.2, http://www.ers.usda.gov/publications/AREI/EIB16/Chapter2/2.2/. Periodically EPA conducts a National Water Quality Inventory that provides a general water quality assessment based on state collected data. The information for the EPA Inventory is for a relatively small subset of the nation's total waters that are assessed by states and does not represent the waterbodies that were not assessed. For additional information, see EPA, *National Water Quality Inventory Report to Congress, 2004 Reporting Cycle*, EPA 841-R-08-001, Washington, DC, January 2009, http://water.epa.gov/lawsregs/guidance/cwa/305b/2004report_index.cfm.

[64] Nonpoint source pollution generally refers to diffuse runoff from farms, ranches, forests and urban areas. Nonpoint sources are also subject to natural variability (e.g., weather related events) and depend on many site-specific conditions, such as topography, soil type, and climate.

[65] Much of the federal response to water quality concerns for agriculture is primarily voluntary and incentive-based.

---

vacated parts of the 2003 rule and remanded other parts to EPA for clarification.[66] The 2008 rule details requirements for permits, annual reports, and development of plans for handling manure and wastewater. Parts of the rule are intended to control land application of manure and agricultural wastewater.

Status

According to EPA, the 2008 rule applies to about 15,300 CAFOs that need permit coverage (74% of the 20,700 CAFOs operating in 2008).[67] Under the rule, CAFOs were to obtain permits and develop and implement nutrient management plans by February 27, 2009.

Further legal challenges followed promulgation of the 2008 revised rule. Agricultural industry groups (although generally satisfied with the rule) filed lawsuits in several federal appellate circuits. Environmental groups also brought a legal challenge to the rule. The various petitions were consolidated in the U.S. Court of Appeals for the 5th Circuit. In addition, EPA officials discussed with environmental plaintiffs possible settlement of portions of the litigation that could involve additional regulatory changes. In December 2009, the court agreed to a joint request from EPA and environmentalists to sever the activists' portion of the litigation. In settling with environmental plaintiffs, EPA agreed to issue guidance aimed at clarifying what CAFOs must do to comply with federal clean water regulations and to help CAFO owners determine whether they need permits; the guidance was issued in May 2010.[68]

In settling that part of the lawsuit, EPA also agreed to propose a rule within one year to collect facility information from all CAFOs, such as number of types of animals, type and capacity of manure storage or treatment process, and quantity of manure generated annually by the CAFO, in order to provide a CAFO inventory and assist in implementing the 2008 rule. In October 2011, EPA proposed a rule, referred to as the CAFO reporting rule, that would require CAFOs to submit a specific set of basic operational information to EPA.[69] The proposal would require CAFOs to provide the following basic information: facility contact information; production area location; whether the CAFO has a CWA permit; the number and type of animals at the CAFO; and the number of acres available for land application of manure, litter, and process wastewater. EPA proposed two reporting options. One option would require every CAFO to report the information to EPA, unless states with authorized CWA programs choose to provide the information on behalf of CAFOs in their state. The second option would require CAFOs in focus watersheds that have water quality concerns associated with CAFOs to report information to EPA. Under the court-

---

[66] U.S. Environmental Protection Agency, "Revised National Pollutant Discharge Elimination System Permit Regulation and Effluent Limitations Guidelines for Concentrated Animal Feeding Operations in Response to the Waterkeeper Decision, Final Rule," 73 *Federal Register* 225, November 20, 2008, pp. 70417-70486. For additional information on EPA's response to the court decision, see CRS Report RL33656, *Animal Waste and Water Quality EPA's Response to the Waterkeeper Alliance Court Decision on Regulation of CAFOs.*

[67] The rule specifies thresholds above which permits are required, such as animal feeding operations that stable or confine more than 700 dairy cows, 2,500 swine weighing 55 pounds or more, or 500 horses.

[68] U.S. Environmental Protection Agency, *Implementation Guidance on CAFO Regulations - CAFOS That Discharge or Are Proposing to Discharge*, EPA-833-R-10-006, May 27, 2010, http://www.epa.gov/npdes/pubs/cafo_implementation_guidance.pdf.

[69] U.S. Environmental Protection Agency, "National Pollutant Discharge Elimination System (NPDES) Concentrated Animal Feeding Operation (CAFO) Reporting Rule; Proposed rule," 76 *Federal Register* 65431-65458, October 21, 2011.

approved agreement with environmental plaintiffs, EPA expects to take final action on a rule by July 2012.

The challenge to the 2008 CAFO rule by agricultural industry groups continued, even after EPA's settlement with environmental plaintiffs. On March 15, 2011, a federal court issued a ruling that supported industry's challenge on several issues. The court upheld the portion of the rule requiring a CAFO to apply for a permit if the facility has an actual discharge. However, the court vacated aspects of the rule requiring permits for proposed discharges (permits are still required for CAFOs that actually discharge) and allowing EPA to take enforcement action against CAFO owners based on their failure to apply for permits.[70]

Issues

The rest of the 2008 rule was not affected by the court's March 2011 ruling and remains in effect. The federal government did not seek a rehearing on the Fifth Circuit's ruling, nor did it petition the Supreme Court for a review. EPA concluded that the court's ruling effectively simplifies permitting by removing uncertainty about the "duty to apply" for a permit and thus is largely self-implementing. The agency has conducted outreach to states on the effect of the ruling and expects at some point to post a disclaimer to the guidance that it issued in May 2010 concerning CAFOs that discharge or propose to discharge.

A number of questions linger about implementation of the 2008 rule. For example, agricultural industry groups are concerned that EPA regions may be providing differing interpretations of a provision of the 2008 rule that allows farms to self-certify that they will not discharge, a finding that allows them to avoid having to apply for a permit and protects CAFOs from liability for not having a permit in the event of an accidental discharge. Some agricultural industry groups also are concerned that EPA could initiate a new rulemaking that would include additional permit and pathogen control requirements.

Separate from the 2008 CAFO rule that applies nationally, EPA is developing new CWA requirements for CAFOs located in the Chesapeake Bay watershed (see "Chesapeake Bay Protection and Restoration," below), which are expected to expand the universe of regulated CAFOs in that region and require more stringent standards for permits. Many in the agriculture sector are concerned that these Chesapeake Bay-specific rules will be the basis for EPA to propose revision of the broader 2008 rule.

Further, EPA's proposed reporting rule has drawn criticism from industry groups who contend that the agency lacks legal authority to require CAFOs that do not discharge to report facility information. Environmental advocates defend EPA's authority to require non-discharging CAFOs to report, but they say that the proposed rule falls short of what is required of EPA under the 2009 settlement agreement that forced the reporting rule.

CRS Contact

Claudia Copeland, Specialist in Resources and Environmental Policy, 7-7227, ccopeland@crs.loc.gov.

---

[70] *National Pork Producers Council v. U.S. EPA*, 635 F.3d 738 (5th Cir. 2011).

Chesapeake Bay Protection and Restoration

Despite several decades of activity by governments, the private sector, and the general public, efforts to improve and protect the Chesapeake Bay watershed have been insufficient to meet restoration goals. Although some specific indicators of Bay health have improved slightly or remained steady (such as blue crabs and underwater bay grasses), others remain at low levels of improvement, especially water quality. Overall, the Bay and its tributaries remain in poor health, with polluted water, reduced populations of fish and shellfish, and degraded habitat and resources. The primary pollutants causing impairments are nutrients (nitrogen and phosphorus) and sediment discharged from multiple urban, suburban, and rural sources around the Bay.

In May 2009, President Obama issued an executive order that declared the Bay a "national treasure" and charged the federal government with assuming a strong leadership role in restoring the Bay.[71] The executive order established a Federal Leadership Committee for the Chesapeake Bay to develop and implement a new strategy for protecting and restoring the Chesapeake region. The resulting strategy, which was released in May 2010, launched major specific environmental initiatives to establish new clean water regulations on stormwater discharges and pollution discharges from animal feedlots in the Bay watershed, put new agricultural conservation practices on farms in the region, and restore land and water habitat.[72]

According to EPA, agriculture represents the single largest source of nutrient and sediment pollution to the Bay, with about half of agriculture's pollutant load directly related to livestock waste. Agriculture covers about 25% of the Bay watershed, and is the largest intensively managed land use in the watershed. EPA believes that excess livestock waste, improperly applied fertilizers, and certain cropland tillage practices increase nutrient and sediment discharges to the Bay.

A central feature of the overall strategy for restoring the Bay is EPA's establishment of a total maximum daily load (TMDL). Section 303 of the CWA requires states to identify waters that are impaired by pollution, even after application of pollution controls. For those waters, states must establish a TMDL to ensure that water quality standards can be attained. A TMDL is essentially a pollution budget, a quantitative estimate of what it takes to achieve standards, setting the maximum amount of pollution that a waterbody can receive without violating standards. If a state fails to do this, EPA is required by the CWA to make its own TMDL determination for the state. Throughout the United States—including the Chesapeake Bay watershed—more than 20,000 waterways are known to be violating applicable water quality standards and to require a TMDL.[73] Lawsuits have been brought with the intention of pressuring EPA and states to develop TMDLs, including for the Chesapeake Bay because the waters of the Bay have been identified as being impaired, that is, as not meeting applicable water quality standards. The Chesapeake Bay TMDL is the largest single TMDL developed to date. It addresses all segments of the Bay and its tidal tributaries that are impaired from discharges of nitrogen, phosphorus, and sediment. The goal is to have TMDL implementation measures in place by 2025 to assure attainment and maintenance of all applicable water quality standards. The TMDL allocates needed reductions of these pollutants

---

[71] Executive Order 13508, "Chesapeake Bay Protection and Restoration," 74 *Federal Register* 23099-23104, May 15, 2009.

[72] For information, see http://www.chesapeakebay.net/news_federalstrategy.aspx?menuitem=51207.

[73] For background information, see CRS Report 97-831, *Clean Water Act and Total Maximum Daily Loads (TMDLs) of Pollutants*.

to all jurisdictions in the 64,000 square mile watershed, not to individual segments of streams or waterbodies, as is more typical of other TMDLs prepared by states or EPA.[74]

As part of the TMDL development process, states are to prepare Watershed Implementation Plans (WIPs) identifying specific reductions and control measures to achieve needed pollutant reductions from point sources (i.e., industrial and municipal facilities and CAFOs) and nonpoint sources (i.e., farms and forests), as well as two-year milestones to implement the plans. EPA fully expects that states will meet commitments and milestones in the WIPs, but the agency also has identified a number of potential actions currently available to it if a state fails to do so, including expanding permit coverage to currently unregulated sources, requiring net improvement offsets, conditioning EPA grants, or increasing federal enforcement in the watershed.

Status

Under a consent decree resolving some of the litigation over the Chesapeake Bay,[75] EPA was required to establish a TMDL no later than May 1, 2011. EPA issued the TMDL on December 29, 2010—ahead of its self-imposed December 31 deadline.[76]

Concurrent with issuance of the TMDL, the Bay watershed jurisdictions (Virginia, Maryland, West Virginia, Delaware, Pennsylvania, and the District of Columbia) prepared Phase I WIPs, which outlined the types of controls and best management practices (BMPs) that will be utilized to achieve the first major goal of the TMDL: that 60% of needed practices to achieve water quality standards will be in place by 2017. The jurisdictions have now developed Phase II WIPs, in which they describe how they will work with specific localities within their borders over the next five years to reduce nitrogen, phosphorus, and sediment loading into streams, lakes, and rivers that feed into the Bay. EPA is reviewing the states' Phase II plans to determine what, if any, extra EPA supervision will be applied in each state.

In the same consent decree that led to issuance of the Bay TMDL, EPA also agreed to revise CWA permit rules for CAFOs located in the Chesapeake Bay watershed (see "Implementation of Existing Clean Water Act Permit Requirements for CAFOs," above). As part of the settlement, EPA agreed to propose Bay-specific rules to expand the universe of regulated CAFOs, including but not limited to designating an AFO as a CAFO or increasing the number of animal operation that would qualify as CAFOs and thus require CWA permits. The settlement also stipulates that EPA will propose more stringent permitting requirements for land application of manure, litter, and process wastewater in the Bay watershed. EPA expects to propose Bay-specific rules by May 2012 and is required by the consent decree to finalize the rules by June 30, 2014.

Issues

EPA's TMDL plans and the overall federal Bay restoration strategy under the 2009 executive order are controversial with agricultural and other groups that are concerned about the likely

---

[74] For information on the TMDL, see http://www.epa.gov/chesapeakebaytmdl/.

[75] *Fowler v. U.S. EPA*, Case No. 1:09-CV-00005-CKK (D.D.C.), May 10, 2010.

[76] Notice of the TMDL appeared in the *Federal Register* January 5, 2011. U.S. Environmental Protection Agency, "Clean Water Act Section 303(d): Notice for the Establishment of the Total Maximum Daily Load (TMDL) for the Chesapeake Bay," 76 *Federal Register* 549-550, January 5, 2011.

mandatory nature of many of EPA's and states' upcoming actions. Agricultural interests are concerned that farm operations in the Bay watershed will be subject to more regulation than competitors in other states, putting their operations at a significant competitive disadvantage. Many of these groups have also been concerned that the underlying scientific data and modeling used by EPA to develop the TMDL do not fully reflect ongoing voluntary efforts by agriculture to reduce pollutant discharges. A lawsuit challenging EPA's authority to set pollution limits under the multistate TMDL was filed by the American Farm Bureau Federation in January 2011.[77] On the other hand, environmental activists in particular are pleased that the federal government is now asserting a leadership role to restore the Bay and have supported legislation that would codify requirements for the Bay TMDL in the CWA, while authorizing grants and other assistance for implementing required measures. Companion bills to do so were introduced in the 111th Congress, while the House Agriculture Committee approved separate legislation (H.R. 5509) that would have authorized an expanded role for USDA in Bay restoration. No legislation was enacted.

The 112th Congress has shown interest in early implementation of the TMDL. The House Agriculture Subcommittee on Conservation, Energy, and Forestry held oversight hearings on March 16 and November 3, 2011. In addition, legislation (H.R. 4153, which is similar to H.R. 5509 in the 111th Congress) has been introduced that would give states, not EPA, authority to set nutrient and sediment limits for the Bay and would increase USDA's role in Bay restoration.

CRS Contact

Claudia Copeland, Specialist in Resources and Environmental Policy, 7-7227, ccopeland@crs.loc.gov.

Florida Nutrient Water Quality Standards

The CWA directs states to adopt water quality standards for their waters and authorizes EPA to promulgate new or revised standards if a state's actions fail to meet CWA requirements. Water quality standards consist of designated uses, criteria to protect the designated uses, and an antidegradation statement. They serve as the framework for pollution control measures that are specified for individual sources by states.

Status

Because of severe water quality impairment of Florida waters by nutrients (nitrogen and phosphorus) from diverse sources, including agriculture and livestock, municipal and industrial wastewater discharges, and urban stormwater runoff, EPA determined in 2009 that Florida's existing *narrative* water quality standards for nutrients must be revised in the form of *numeric* criteria that will enable Florida to better control nutrient pollution. In 2009 EPA entered into a consent decree with environmental litigants requiring the agency to promulgate numeric nutrient water quality standards for Florida. To meet the legal deadline, EPA issued the first phase of these standards on November 15, 2010, establishing standards for lakes and flowing waters in the state. The EPA rule does not establish any requirements directly applicable to regulated entities or other

---

[77] *American Farm Bureau Federation and Pennsylvania Farm Bureau v. U.S. EPA*, Case No. 11-cv-0067 (United States District Court for the Middle District of Pennsylvania 2011).

sources of nutrient pollution. Water quality standards do not have the force of law until the state translates them into permit limits or otherwise imposes pollution control requirements on dischargers in the state.[78]

The rule has not yet gone into effect, as EPA has delayed the effective date to prepare for implementation and state efforts to develop a rule that EPA could approve. First, in response to criticism of the proposed standards, EPA delayed the effective date of the 2010 rule for 15 months, to allow local governments, businesses, and the state of Florida time to review the standards and develop implementation strategies.

Second, EPA has said all along that it prefers that Florida implement its own numeric nutrient water quality criteria, and in recent months, the state has been developing such standards. EPA has preliminarily indicated that, if these standards are submitted to the federal agency for final approval, EPA likely would approve them, at which time the agency would initiate administrative action to repeal the 2010 federal rule. To that end, in March EPA delayed the effective date of the 2010 rule until July 6, 2012, to allow the state to complete its process and to avoid confusion that could occur if federal criteria became effective while state criteria are being reviewed.

At the same time, separate legal challenges to the rule were filed in federal court by environmental advocates, several industry groups, and Florida's agriculture commissioners. In February, a federal court ruling largely upheld EPA's authority and methodology in setting numeric criteria for nutrient pollution in Florida waters, but remanded a portion of the rule concerning numeric criteria for streams, saying they were arbitrary and capricious.[79]

Even while state officials submit their rule for streams, lakes, spring and estuaries to EPA for approval, the agency continues crafting a rule for the second phase of standards—for Southern Florida inland flowing waters, and estuarine and costal waters—which is due to be proposed by May 21, 2012, and finalized by January 7, 2013.

Issues

While few dispute the need to reduce nutrients in Florida's waters, EPA's rule has been controversial, involving disputes about the data underlying the proposal, potential costs of complying with numeric standards when they are incorporated into discharge permit limitations, and disputes over administrative flexibility. EPA responds that the rule is intended to ensure the health of Florida's waterways and its economy, because the types of water quality problems associated with nutrients—algae blooms that are toxic to humans, fish, and animals—have economic impacts throughout the state.

EPA estimated that the potential incremental costs associated with the rule range from $16 million to $25 million per year, and estimated monetized benefits of $28 million per year. Many stakeholders contend that EPA has greatly underestimated costs. In response to these criticisms, EPA agreed to ask the National Academy of Sciences to conduct an independent review of the rule's implementation cost. The requested report was released in March.[80] The committee found

---

[78] U.S. Environmental Protection Agency, "Water Quality Standards for the State of Florida's Lakes and Flowing Waters; Final Rule," 75 *Federal Register* 75762-75807, December 5, 2010.

[79] *Florida Wildlife Federation v. Jackson*, N.D. Fla., No. 4:08-cv-00324, Feb. 18, 2012.

[80] Water Science and Technology Board, Division on Earth and Life Sciences, National Research Council of the (continued...)

that EPA underestimated the cost of implementing the rule and questioned the validity of several assumptions in EPA's cost analysis. In particular, it found that the agency did not adequately report on uncertainties that would affect the cost of changing from narrative to numeric water quality standards. Members of the committee noted that a major factor in the wide range of cost estimates was the approach taken by differing parties. EPA focused on the increase in cost from narrative to numeric standards, not total costs, while some other stakeholder groups sought to estimate not incremental costs, but at least some fraction of total costs, making comparisons difficult. The report did not attempt to project the costs of the EPA or alternative rule.

Some groups also fear that EPA's actions in Florida, which represented the first time that EPA has established statewide numeric nutrient standards, will be a precedent for similar regulatory action elsewhere. For example, environmental advocacy groups have petitioned or filed lawsuits seeking to require EPA to establish numeric nutrient water quality standards in Kansas and for the Mississippi River Basin.[81] In testimony before the House Agriculture Committee in March 2011, EPA Administrator Jackson stated that EPA is not working on any federal numeric nutrient limits, and the agency has developed guidance for its regional offices stating that addressing nutrient pollution is a problem best handled by states through a variety of tools.[82]

These issues also have drawn Congress's attention. In 2011, oversight hearings were held by subcommittees of the House Energy and Commerce and Transportation and Infrastructure committees, and legislation has been introduced to limit EPA's authority to promulgate numeric nutrient criteria in Florida (S. 2115/H.R. 3856).

CRS Contact

Claudia Copeland, Specialist in Resources and Environmental Policy, 7-7227, ccopeland@crs.loc.gov.

Spill Prevention, Control, and Countermeasure (SPCC) Plans

The CWA mandated regulations to prevent the discharge of oil from various sources.[83] Pursuant to this statutory requirement,[84] EPA crafted regulations for non-transportation-related facilities in 1973. Affected facilities must prepare and implement spill prevention control and countermeasure (SPCC) plans.[85] For example, SPCC regulations require secondary containment (e.g., dikes or

---

(...continued)

National Academies, *Review of the EPA's Economic Analysis of Final Water Quality Standards for Nutrients for Lakes and Flowing Waters in Florida*, March 2012, http://www.nap.edu/catalog.php?record_id=13376.

[81] In July 2011, EPA denied the petition requesting that EPA promulgate national numeric nutrient criteria for the United States or, alternatively, for waters of the Mississippi-Atchafalaya River Basin and northern Gulf of Mexico, saying, "We do not believe that the comprehensive use of federal rulemaking authority is the most effective or practical means of addressing these concerns at this time."

[82] "EPA Nutrient Reduction Framework Urges States to Develop Plan, Schedule for Criteria," *Daily Environment Report*, March 17, 2011, p. A-16.

[83] Section 311(j)(1) of CWA.

[84] And in accordance with Executive Order 11735 (August 3, 1973), granting EPA the authority to regulate non-transportation-related onshore and offshore facilities.

[85] U.S. Environmental Protection Agency, "Oil Pollution Prevention: Non-Transportation Related Onshore and Offshore Facilities," *Federal Register*, vol. 38, no. 237 (December 11, 1973), pp. 34164-34170.

---

berms) for certain oil-storage units; and plans must be certified by a Professional Engineer unless a facility owner/operator is able to self-certify the plan.

The EPA SPCC plan requirements apply to non-transportation-related facilities that drill, produce, store, process, refine, transfer, distribute, use, or consume oil or oil products;[86] and that could reasonably be expected to discharge oil to U.S. navigable waters or adjoining shorelines.[87] Facilities, including farms,[88] are subject to the rule if they meet at least one of the following capacity thresholds: an aboveground aggregate oil storage capacity greater than 1,320 U.S. gallons,[89] or a completely buried oil storage capacity greater than 42,000 U.S. gallons.

Status

Following the passage of the Oil Pollution Act of 1990,[90] EPA proposed substantial changes and clarifications to the SPCC regulations that were made final in July 2002.[91] EPA has both extended the 2002 rule's compliance date (on multiple occasions) and made further amendments to the 2002 rule.[92] For most types of facilities subject to SPCC requirements, the deadline for complying with the changes made in 2002 was November 10, 2011.[93] However, in a November 20, 2011, rule, EPA extended the compliance date for farms to May 10, 2013.[94]

Note that the July 2002 final rule and subsequent amendments do not alter the requirement for owners or operators of facilities in operation before August 16, 2002—the effective date of the 2002 final rule—to maintain and to continue implementing their SPCC plans in accordance with the SPCC regulations in effect before the 2002 rulemaking.

Issues

Some of the recent SPCC rulemakings have included provisions that would affect agricultural operations. One issue that has received interest is the applicability of the SPCC requirements to

---

[86] Per EPA SPCC regulations, "oil," means oil of any kind or in any form, including, but not limited to: petroleum; fuel oil; sludge; oil refuse; oil mixed with wastes other than dredged spoil; fats, oils or greases of animal, fish, or marine mammal origin; vegetable oils, including oil from seeds, nuts, fruits, or kernels; and other oils and greases, including synthetic oils and mineral oils. 40 C.F.R. §112.2.

[87] Some of the definitions for the terms used to determine SPCC applicability may be subject to interpretation. For example, the definition of "navigable waters" has been a subject of debate and litigation in recent years. See CRS Report RL33263, *The Wetlands Coverage of the Clean Water Act (CWA) Is Revisited by the Supreme Court Rapanos v. United States.*

[88] Although the definition of facility does not specifically mention farms, farms are explicitly defined as "a facility on a tract of land devoted to the production of crops or raising of animals, including fish, which produced and sold, or normally would have produced and sold, $1,000 or more of agricultural products during a year." See 40 C.F.R. §112.2.

[89] Only counting containers greater than 55 gallons. 40 C.F.R. §112.1(d).

[90] P.L. 101-380; 33 U.S.C. §2701 *et seq.*

[91] U.S. Environmental Protection Agency, "Oil Pollution Prevention and Response; Non-Transportation-Related Onshore and Offshore Facilities: Final Rule," 67 *Federal Register* 47041, July 17, 2002.

[92] These actions were, at least in part, related to legal challenges that followed the 2002 final rule.

[93] U.S. Environmental Protection Agency, "Oil Pollution Prevention; Spill Prevention, Control, and Countermeasure Rule Compliance Date Amendment ," 75 Federal Register 63093, October 14, 2010.

[94] U.S. Environmental Protection Agency, "Oil Pollution Prevention: Spill Prevention, Control, and Countermeasure Rule—Compliance Date Amendment for Farms," 76 Federal Register 72120, November 22, 2011.

---

milk containers.[95] Pursuant to the CWA definition of oil, the SPCC requirements apply to petroleum-based and non-petroleum-based oil.[96] In a 1975 *Federal Register* notice, EPA clarified that its 1973 SPCC regulations apply to oils from animal and vegetable sources.[97] EPA subsequently stated that "milk typically contains a percentage of animal fat, which is a non-petroleum oil" and is thus subject to SPCC provisions.[98] However, EPA issued a final rule April 18, 2011, exempting all milk and milk product containers and associated piping from the SPCC requirements. EPA's rationale for the exemption is that these units are subject to industry standards for sanitation and construction and may be regulated by other agencies, including the USDA.[99] In addition, the final rule states that exempted milk storage units are not included in a facility's overall oil storage volume, a primary factor for SPCC applicability.

In some cases, EPA appears to have taken different approaches to farms over time. For example, in a December 2006 final rule, EPA decided to extend the SPCC plan compliance date for small farms (i.e., total oil storage capacity of 10,000 gallons or less) "either indefinitely or until the Agency publishes a final rule in the *Federal Register* establishing a new compliance date."[100] EPA removed this provision in a June 2009 final rule, establishing the same compliance dates for farms as for all other facilities. In addition, in its December 5, 2008, rulemaking,[101] EPA specifically excluded farms from the loading/unloading rack requirements.[102] However, in its November 2009 final rule, EPA removed this exclusion, concluding that "certain facilities (i.e., farms and oil production facilities) should not be treated differently than other facilities, even if loading/unloading racks are not typically associated with these types of facilities."[103]

However, the most recent substantive rulemaking, in November 2009, included some amendments that may benefit farming operations. The rule exempts pesticide application equipment and related mix containers that may currently be subject to the SPCC rule when crop oil or adjuvant oil are added to formulations. EPA also clarifies that a nurse tank is considered a mobile refueler, and, like other types of mobile refuelers, is exempt from the sized secondary containment requirements. EPA estimated that the total cost savings to farm owners and operators from these (and other) amendments amount to $13 million on an annualized basis (2007$).[104]

---

[95] As of the date of this report, Members of Congress have introduced at least one proposal addressing this issue (e.g., S. 104, introduced by Senator Johanns January 25, 2011).

[96] See CWA §311(a) (33 U.S.C. 1321(a)).

[97] U.S. Environmental Protection Agency, "'Oil Pollution Prevention, Applicability of 40 CFR part 112 to Non-Petroleum Oils; Notice," 40 *Federal Register* 28849, July 9, 1975.

[98] U.S. Environmental Protection Agency, "Oil Pollution Prevention; Spill Prevention, Control, and Countermeasure Rule Requirements—Amendments," 74 *Federal Register* 2461, January 15, 2009.

[99] U.S. Environmental Protection Agency, "Oil Pollution Prevention; Spill Prevention, Control, and Countermeasure (SPCC) Rule—Amendments for Milk and Milk Product Containers," 76 *Federal Register* 21652, April 18, 2011.

[100] U.S. Environmental Protection Agency, "Oil Pollution Prevention; Spill Prevention, Control, and Countermeasure Plan Requirements – Amendment: Final Rule," 71 *Federal Register* 77266, December 26, 2006.

[101] On December 5, 2008, EPA amended the SPCC rule to clarify certain provisions (U.S. Environmental Protection Agency, "Oil Pollution Prevention; Spill Prevention, Control, and Countermeasure Rule Requirements—Amendments: Final Rule," 73 *Federal Register* 74236, December 5, 2008.). These requirements were to become effective on February 3, 2009. However, the incoming Obama Administration delayed the effective date of the December 2008 rulemaking for regulatory review.

[102] 40 C.F.R. §112.7(h).

[103] U.S. Environmental Protection Agency, "Oil Pollution Prevention; Spill Prevention, Control, and Countermeasure (SPCC) Rule - Amendments," 74 *Federal Register* 58784, November 13, 2009.

[104] Ibid, p. 58805.

CRS Contact

Jonathan Ramseur, Specialist in Environmental Policy, 7-7919, jramseur@crs.loc.gov.

Energy

The agricultural industry is sensitive to fluctuations in energy sources and cost. The use of fossil fuel-based fertilizers, diesel fuel, and, more recently, corn-based ethanol all have a significant impact on both crop and livestock operations. Since the 1970s, federal policies have offered a variety of incentives, regulations, and programs to encourage growth in the bioenergy industry as a sustainable alternative to fossil fuels.[105] The increased emphasis on agriculture-based biofuels has received mixed reviews within the agricultural community.[106] While some continue to push for greater federal involvement, critics of the federal intervention also have emerged.

The following section covers several federal regulations relating to energy, including:

- motor vehicle and heavy-duty truck greenhouse gas (GHG) rule and Corporate Average Fuel Economy (CAFE) standards;

- renewable fuels standard (RFS2) rule; and

- E15 waiver petition.

Motor Vehicle and Heavy-Duty Truck GHG Rule and Corporate Average Fuel Economy (CAFE) Standards

The Energy Policy and Conservation Act of 1975 (EPCA)[107] requires car and light truck manufacturers to meet corporate average fuel economy (CAFE) standards. The Energy Independence and Security Act of 2007 (EISA)[108] requires the National Highway Traffic Safety Administration (NHTSA) to develop rules to tighten CAFE standards and to promulgate fuel economy standards for medium- and heavy-duty trucks, reflecting the "maximum feasible improvement" in fuel efficiency.

In response to a 2007 Supreme Court decision (*Massachusetts v. EPA*),[109] EPA is required to, among other things, determine whether GHGs from automobiles endanger public health and welfare. On December 7, 2009, EPA issued such an "Endangerment Finding." Thus, under the Clean Air Act (CAA), EPA is required to promulgate rules on emissions of GHGs from motor vehicles. Because fuel economy and vehicle GHG emissions are tightly linked, the

---

[105] For more information on agriculture-based biofuels, see CRS Report R41282, *Agriculture-Based Biofuels Overview and Emerging Issues*.

[106] Examples of agriculture-based biofuels policy proponents include organizations who currently benefit directly from policies, such as the National Corn Growers Association (corn-based ethanol) and American Soybean Association (soybean-based biodiesel). Critics include organizations who rely on current biofuel sources for other non-fuel purposes, such as the National Cattleman's Beef Association and National Pork Producers Council.

[107] P.L. 94-163.

[108] P.L. 110-140.

[109] See CRS Report RS22665, *The Supreme Court's Climate Change Decision Massachusetts v. EPA*.

Administration proposed light-duty vehicle regulations in September 2009 that would integrate fuel economy and GHG rules into one process;[110] regulations for model year (MY) 2012-MY2016 were finalized in May 2010[111] and in October 2010 EPA and NHTSA announced their intent to propose similar regulations for MY2017-2025.[112] On November 30, 2010, EPA and NHTSA proposed integrated GHG and fuel economy standards for medium-and heavy-duty vehicles.[113]

Status

On May 7, 2010, EPA and NHTSA finalized rules to integrate CAFE standards with light-duty vehicle GHG standards. The Administration estimates that the rule will reduce lifecycle costs for most vehicle purchasers, as fuel savings are expected to more than offset the increase in purchase price ($1,100). The new standards will be phased in beginning with MY2012. While the rulemaking process was combined, EPA and NHTSA have recognized that some parts of the GHG program will not translate to the CAFE program, and vice versa.[114]

In October 2010 EPA and NHTSA announced their intent to propose further regulations for MY2017-MY2025,[115] and on July 29, 2011, the agencies announced an agreement with California and 13 automakers on the framework of new regulations to be formally proposed in the fall of 2011.[116]

EPA's endangerment finding specifically referenced medium- and heavy-duty trucks as among sources that contribute to GHG emissions. On August 9, 2011, EPA and NHTSA finalized heavy-duty truck GHG and fuel economy standards that will be phased in between 2014 and 2018.[117] EPA and NHTSA estimate that the rules will reduce lifecycle vehicle costs, factoring in the fuel

---

[110] U.S. Environmental Protection Agency and National Highway Traffic Safety Administration, "Proposed Rulemaking to Establish Light-Duty Vehicle Greenhouse Gas Emission Standards and Corporate Average Fuel Economy Standards; Proposed Rule," 74 *Federal Register* 49454-49789, September 28, 2009.

[111] U.S. Environmental Protection Agency and National Highway Traffic Safety Administration, "Light-Duty Vehicle Greenhouse Gas Emission Standards and Corporate Average Fuel Economy Standards; Final Rule," 75 *Federal Register* 25324-25728, May 7, 2010.

[112] U.S. Environmental Protection Agency and National Highway Traffic Safety Administration, "2017 and Later Model Year Light Duty Vehicle GHG Emissions and CAFE Standards; Notice of Intent," 75 *Federal Register* 62739-62750, October 13, 2010.

[113] U.S. Environmental Protection Agency and National Highway Traffic Safety Administration, "Greenhouse Gas Emissions Standards and Fuel Efficiency Standards for Medium- and Heavy-Duty Engines and Vehicles; Proposed Rule," 75 *Federal Register* 74152-74456, November 30, 2010.

[114] U.S. Environmental Protection Agency and National Highway Traffic Safety Administration, "Proposed Rulemaking to Establish Light-Duty Vehicle Greenhouse Gas Emission Standards and Corporate Average Fuel Economy Standards; Proposed Rule," 74 *Federal Register* 49468, September 28, 2009.

[115] U.S. Environmental Protection Agency and National Highway Traffic Safety Administration, "2017 and Later Model Year Light Duty Vehicle GHG Emissions and CAFE Standards; Notice of Intent," 75 *Federal Register* 62739-62750, October 13, 2010.

[116] U.S. Environmental Protection Agency and National Highway Traffic Safety Administration, "2017-2025 Model Year Light-Duty Vehicle GHG Emissions and CAFE Standards: Supplemental Notice of Intent," 76 *Federal Register* 48758, August 9, 2011.

[117] U.S. Environmental Protection Agency and National Highway Traffic Safety Administration, *Greenhouse Gas Emissions Standards and Fuel Efficiency Standards for Medium- and Heavy-Duty Engines and Vehicles Final Rules,* EPA-HQ-OAR-2010-0162, Washington, DC, August 9, 2011, http://www.epa.gov/otaq/climate/documents/ghg-hd-rule.pdf.

savings and increase in purchase price.[118] EPA estimates that, because of fuel savings, most truck owners would see a payback period of one to five years.[119]

Issues

This issue has a somewhat indirect effect on agriculture. The fact that vehicle purchase prices are expected to increase may affect agricultural producers who purchase cars, light trucks, and heavy trucks for use in their businesses (including light-duty and super-duty pickups, vans, and flatbed trucks). While for most purchasers those increases will be offset by lower fuel expenditures over the lifetime of these vehicles, the increase in up-front costs may influence some agricultural producers' decisions to purchase new vehicles notwithstanding the expected lifecycle cost savings. The proposed heavy-duty rules do not directly apply to non-road engines and equipment, but because many heavy-duty diesel engines are used in both on-road and non-road applications (including farm equipment), some stakeholders are concerned that compliance with rules could raise the cost of diesel engines in general.

CRS Contact

Brent Yacobucci, Specialist in Energy and Environmental Policy, 7-9662, byacobucci@crs.loc.gov.

Renewable Fuels Standard (RFS2) Rule

The Energy Independence and Security Act (EISA) expanded the renewable fuel standard (RFS) established in the Energy Policy Act of 2005.[120] On February 3, 2010, EPA finalized new rules for the expanded renewable fuel standard (RFS2).[121] The RFS requires a significant growth in U.S. biofuel use. In 2012, the RFS mandate is 15.2 billion gallons of biofuels from various sources (consisting mostly of ethanol from corn starch). By 2022, EISA will require that 36 billion gallons of biofuel be used in the nation's fuel supply. Within the larger RFS, EISA mandates the growing use of advanced biofuels (i.e., non-corn starch ethanol), including fuels produced from cellulosic feedstocks. By 2022, the advanced biofuels mandate grows to 21 billion gallons, including 16 billion gallons of cellulosic biofuel.[122]

EISA also requires that advanced biofuels—e.g., cellulosic biofuels, biomass-based diesel substitutes, and other advanced biofuels—as well as conventional biofuels from newly built

---

[118] In MY2008, EPA estimates a purchase price increase of $400 for vocational trucks, $1,400 for heavy-duty pickups and vans, and $6,200 for combination tractors (tractor-trailers).

[119] U.S. Environmental Protection Agency, *EPA and NHTSA Propose First-Ever Program to Reduce Greenhouse Gas Emissions and Improve Fuel Efficiency of Medium- and Heavy-Duty Vehicles: Regulatory Announcement*, EPA-420-F-10-901, Washington, DC, October 2010, http://www.epa.gov/otaq/climate/regulations/420f10901.htm.

[120] P.L. 109-58.

[121] Environmental Protection Agency, *Regulation of Fuels and Fuel Additives Changes to Renewable Fuel Standard Program*, EPA-HQ-OAR-2005-0161, Washington, DC, February 3, 2010, http://www.epa.gov/otaq/renewablefuels/rfs2-preamble.pdf.

[122] For more information, see CRS Report R40168, *Alternative Fuels and Advanced Technology Vehicles Issues in Congress*.

---

refineries, meet certain lifecycle GHG reduction requirements.[123] EPA is required to classify biofuel production based on their lifecycle emissions, including emissions from direct and indirect changes in land use. Only fuels that achieve a 50% reduction in GHG emissions relative to petroleum fuels may be classified as advanced biofuels. Cellulosic biofuels must achieve at least a 60% GHG emission reduction, while fuels from new corn ethanol plants must achieve a 20% GHG emission reduction—corn ethanol plants in existence or under construction when EISA was enacted (December 19, 2007) are grandfathered.

Status

Under the Clean Air Act Section 211(o), as amended by EISA, EPA is required to set the annual standards under the RFS based on gasoline and diesel projections from the Energy Information Administration (EIA). EPA is also required to set the cellulosic biofuel standard each year based on the volume projected to be available during the following year, using EIA projections and assessments of production capability from industry.[124] For 2012, the RFS2 requires the use of 15.2 billion gallons of ethanol and other biofuels in transportation fuel. Within the larger mandate, the RFS2 requires the use of 2.0 billion gallons of advanced biofuels (fuels other than corn starch ethanol) in 2012, including 8.65 million gallons of cellulosic biofuels. Within the rules, EPA finalized procedures for fuel suppliers to generate credits under the system—credits that can be sold or traded. EPA also finalized methodologies for determining lifecycle GHG emissions.

Issues

The RFS has been a major policy supporting the development of U.S. biofuels industries, especially for corn-based ethanol producers. Many believe that the expanded RFS2 will be the main pillar of support for existing U.S. biodiesel production capacity (due to the uneconomical nature of U.S. biodiesel production). In future years, as the advanced biofuel mandates grow, the RFS could be the key driver for the development of biofuels from cellulose, algae, and other non-food/feed commodities.

RFS expansion has contributed to concomitant pressure on limited agricultural resources (most notably land) as feedstock production has intensified on existing cropland and expanded onto new, marginal lands. This has raised the general price level for those commodities that compete for the affected cropland, as well as having important secondary effects in related agricultural markets, including livestock feed markets and agricultural input markets. As a result, the potential for unintended consequences (e.g., land use, commodity prices) in non-biofuels markets could remain important unless or until crop yields catch up to and/or exceed biofuels' mandated growth under the RFS.

Expanding cultivation onto marginal lands (including reclaimed Conservation Reserve Program acres) and more intensive cultivation (including increased water, pesticide, and fertilizer use) on existing cropland has put new pressures on environmental resources. This has put substantial

---

[123] For more information, see CRS Report R40460, *Calculation of Lifecycle Greenhouse Gas Emissions for the Renewable Fuel Standard (RFS)*.

[124] "EPA Finalizes 2012 Renewable Fuel Standards," Office of Transportation and Air Quality, EPA-420-F-11-044, December 2011.

pressure on the agricultural research infrastructure to develop technologies or techniques that enhance per-acre productivity in an effort to mitigate unintended price pressures and secondary market effects.

The clearest example of increasing pressure on resources (with unintended consequences) is the rapid growth of corn use for ethanol production. During the 2005/2006 crop year, corn ethanol production used 1.6 billion bushels of corn, or about 14.4% of U.S. production. This usage share has grown in lockstep with the RFS mandate. In the current 2011/2012 crop year, corn ethanol production is expected to approach 13.8 billion gallons, while consuming over 5 billion bushels, or nearly 40% of the 2011 corn harvest.[125] While U.S. corn production has expanded and is expected to continue to expand (primarily due to continued yield growth, as corn area expansion is thought to be very near its sustainable maximum), corn use for ethanol has expanded even faster. As a result, corn prices have moved steadily higher. The 2005/2006 crop year farm price for corn was $2.00 per bushel. The farm price of corn was $4.20 per bushel in 2007/2008 and $5.18 in 2010/2011, and is projected at $6.20 in 2011/2012.[126] Corn is the primary feed ingredient used by the U.S. livestock sector, representing over 90% of all grains consumed, and about 57% of all grains and feed concentrates consumed annually. As the price of corn rises, the entire feed complex price structure has risen, putting a cost squeeze on the U.S. livestock sector. In the long run, an intensification of this pressure could lead to regional shifts in comparative advantage of certain livestock production activities that could increasingly favor proximity to corn ethanol plants for access to the co-product distiller's dried grains and solubles.

Corn ethanol production is approaching its ceiling of 15 billion gallons by 2015. As a result, its impact in other corn-user markets is expected to diminish in the coming years. The effect of the "blend wall" (see "E15 Waiver Petition" discussion, below) in constraining the commercial use of ethanol this past year heralds the eventual mitigation of biofuels' spillover impact in secondary markets. However, current tight corn supplies and the uncertainty of planting and harvesting this year's crop are likely to keep upward pressure on commodity prices. If a near-term corn supply shortfall were to develop, policymakers could feel tremendous pressure to waive future RFS mandates.

Another key issue is the role of cellulosic biofuels in the RFS2. Cellulosic biofuels are in their infancy, and commercial development has been slow. As of early 2012, no commercial-scale refinery had yet begun operation.[127] Because of this, EPA had to use its waiver authority under EISA to reduce the mandate for the first three years of implementation: the 2010 level for cellulosic biofuels was lowered from 100 million gallons to 6.5 million gallons (a decrease of over 90%); for 2011, EPA reduced the cellulosic mandate from 250 million gallons (as scheduled in EISA) down to 6.6 million gallons; and for 2012 it was lowered from the scheduled 500 million gallons to 8.65 million gallons.[128] It is unclear what effect the delays in implementing the cellulosic biofuel mandate will have on investment and in the development of the cellulosic biofuel industry.

---

[125] World Agricultural Outlook Board, *World Agricultural Supply and Demand Estimates (WASDE)*, March 9, 2012.

[126] Mid-point of the projected season average farm price range of $4.90 to $5.70 per bushel, *WASDE*, November 9, 2011.

[127] For more information, see CRS Report RL34738, *Cellulosic Biofuels Analysis of Policy Issues for Congress.*

[128] Environmental Protection Agency, "Regulation of Fuels and Fuel Additives; 2011 Renewable Fuel Standards," 75 *Federal Register* 76790-76830, December 9, 2010.

CRS Contacts

Brent Yacobucci, Specialist in Energy and Environmental Policy, 7-9662, byacobucci@crs.loc.gov, or Randy Schnepf, Specialist in Agricultural Policy, 7-4277, rschnepf@crs.loc.gov.

E15 Waiver Petition

By 2022, EISA requires the use of 36 billion gallons of renewable fuels, and much of this could be ethanol from a variety of feedstocks (many of which are agricultural-based; see "Renewable Fuels Standard (RFS2) Rule" discussion, above). However, there is an obstacle to the use of this quantity of ethanol in gasoline. Currently, although some ethanol is sold as an alternative fuel (E85), most is sold as an additive in conventional and reformulated gasoline. Until recently, the amount of ethanol that could be blended into gasoline for all uses was limited to 10% by volume (E10) pursuant to EPA guidance under the CAA, as well as by vehicle and engine warranties, and certification procedures for fuel-dispensing equipment.

As the RFS is structured, assuming that most of the mandate is met using ethanol, the volume of ethanol blended in gasoline is limited by gasoline consumption. In 2012, the RFS will require over 15 billion gallons of renewable fuel, while projected gasoline consumption in 2012 is 138 billion gallons. After 2012, the renewable fuel mandate will continue to increase. However, a limit of 10% ethanol means that ethanol for gasoline blending (not including E85) likely cannot exceed 14 billion gallons per year. This "blend wall" is the maximum possible volume of ethanol that can be blended into U.S. motor gasoline. The actual limit could be slightly lower, since older fuel tanks and pumps at some retail stations may not be equipped to handle ethanol-blended fuel.[129]

Status

On March 6, 2009, Growth Energy (on behalf of 52 U.S. ethanol producers) applied to EPA for a waiver from the CAA limitation on ethanol content in gasoline. Until recently, ethanol content in gasoline for all uses was capped at 10% (E10); the application requested an increase in the maximum concentration to 15% (E15). If fully granted, the waiver would allow the use of significantly more ethanol in gasoline than is currently permitted.

On November 4, 2010, EPA granted a partial waiver allowing the use of E15 in MY2007 and newer vehicles.[130] The agency delayed a decision on MY2001-MY2006 vehicles until the Department of Energy completed testing of those vehicles. On January 21, 2011, EPA announced that the waiver would be expanded to include MY2001-MY2006 vehicles.[131] EPA determined that data were insufficient to address concerns that had been raised over emissions from MY2000 and

---

[129] For more information see CRS Report R40445, *Intermediate-Level Blends of Ethanol in Gasoline, and the Ethanol "Blend Wall"*.

[130] Environmental Protection Agency, "Partial Grant and Partial Denial of Clean Air Act Waiver Application Submitted by Growth Energy to Increase the Allowable Ethanol Content of Gasoline to 15 Percent; Decision of the Administrator; Notice," 75 *Federal Register* 68094-68150, November 4, 2010.

[131] Environmental Protection Agency, "Partial Grant of Clean Air Act Waiver Application Submitted by Growth Energy to Increase the Allowable Ethanol Content of Gasoline to 15 Percent; Decision of the Administrator," signed January 21, 2011 (awaiting publication in the *Federal Register*).

older vehicles, as well as heavy-duty vehicles, motorcycles, and non-road applications (including farm equipment), and thus a waiver for these vehicles/engines was denied. EPA has noted that granting the waiver eliminates only one impediment to the use of E15—other factors, including retail and blending infrastructure (including gasoline storage tanks and pumps), state and local laws and regulations, and manufacturers' warranties, would still need to be addressed. Because of concerns over potential damage by E15 to equipment not designed for its use, this partial waiver has been challenged in court by a group of vehicle and engine manufacturers.[132] On February 19, 2011, the House adopted an amendment to H.R. 1 (H.Amdt. 156) that would block EPA from using FY2011 funds to implement the agency's waiver decision. However, on March 15, EPA approved the model misfueling mitigation plan (MMP) submitted by the Renewable Fuels Association (RFA) as step for companies to develop their own MMPs.[133] The next steps for companies seeking to offer E15 will include ensuring that the companies are registered with EPA, that companies have submitted the MMP, and that companies are addressing lingering fuel regulatory requirement at the state level.

Issues

EPA approval of the waiver request could help open the door to E15 blending. This could be a strong signal to the biofuels industry concerning federal support for meeting and enforcing RFS mandate levels. As a result, this could help to stimulate new investment in the biofuels sector. In the short run, the corn ethanol industry would be the main beneficiary, since it is best able to respond to the expanding RFS mandates. Any further increase in corn ethanol use would benefit corn producers. The net result would be an intensification of agricultural resource use with the same consequences discussed previously (see "Renewable Fuels Standard (RFS2) Rule").

The ability to address concerns over the use of E15 in legacy equipment (both infrastructure and vehicles) will affect the rollout of E15 to retail stations. As noted above, EPA's decision to allow E15 in some vehicles only addresses one part of the blend wall. State laws and regulations, vehicle and equipment certifications and warranties, and questions over fuel suppliers willingness to market the fuel could all be impediments to an expansion of E15 use. The result of equipment manufacturers' legal challenge to the partial wavier will be a key factor.

CRS Contacts

Brent Yacobucci, Specialist in Energy and Environmental Policy, 7-9662, byacobucci@crs.loc.gov, or Randy Schnepf, Specialist in Agricultural Policy, 7-4277, rschnepf@crs.loc.gov.

---

[132] The Alliance of Automobile Manufacturers (Alliance), the Association of International Automobile Manufacturers, Inc. (AIAM), the National Marine Manufacturers Association (NMMA), and the Outdoor Power Equipment Institute (OPEI). OPEI, Fact Sheet: E-15 Partial Waiver Legal Challenge, December 17, 2010. The case is *Alliance of Automobile Manufacturers et. al v. Environmental Protection Agency.*

[133] Renewable Fuels Association News Release, "Ethanol Industry, EPA Ready for E15 Rollout," March 15, 2012; available at http://www.ethanolrfa.org/news/entry/ethanol-industry-epa-ready-for-e15-rollout/.

Chemicals

Agricultural "pests" can interfere with the production of crops and livestock used for food and fiber. Pests may include insects, plant pathogens, weeds, and vertebrates. If in abundance, pests may affect crop yield and cause a decline in quality. Hundreds of chemical products are available to repel or kill pests that affect agricultural production. Each uses different active ingredients, has a different potency, and has a different impact on human health and the environment. The federal regulation of these chemicals includes registering and restricting their use.

The following section covers five federal regulations relating to chemicals, including:

- disclosure of pesticide inert ingredients;
- Clean Water Act permits for pesticide application;
- pesticide drift labeling;
- Atrazine; and
- the Endangered Species Act (ESA).

Disclosure of Pesticide Inert Ingredients

Pesticide products generally contain active ingredients that are intended to control targeted pests as well as inert ingredients that are included to dilute the active ingredients, increase their ability to penetrate or adhere to leaf surfaces, or otherwise aid in the distribution and effectiveness of the pesticide product. Inert ingredients are not "active ingredients," but they are not necessarily chemically inert. Some inerts are potentially toxic or otherwise hazardous.

The Federal Insecticide, Fungicide, and Rodenticide Act (FIFRA) directs EPA to regulate the sale and use of pesticide products and pesticide labels by establishing requirements for pesticide labels. Use of a pesticide in a manner that is inconsistent with label instructions is a violation of FIFRA. One requirement for pesticide labels is a listing of active ingredients. No listing is required for most inert ingredients, but labels must indicate the total percentage of the product that is inert.

EPA has received two petitions requesting disclosure of certain potentially hazardous inert ingredients on pesticide labels. One petition was from 22 nongovernmental organizations, while the other was from the attorneys general of 15 U.S. states and territories. The petitioners requested that EPA require disclosure of certain inert ingredients that have been designated as hazardous under other environmental statutes. In response to the petitions, EPA is considering regulatory and voluntary options for providing information to the public about the identities of inert ingredients in pesticide products. According to EPA, it has the authority to require disclosure if the Administrator "determines that such ingredient(s) may pose a hazard to man or the environment."[134] In 1987, EPA required disclosure on pesticide labels of the identities of

---

[134] 40 C.F.R. §156.10(g)(7).

approximately 50 "inerts of toxicological concern."[135] A future rulemaking might expand this disclosure requirement to hundreds of additional chemicals and mixtures.

Status

In response to petitions, EPA issued an advanced notice of proposed rulemaking on December 23, 2009.[136] Comments on options for providing public information closed on April 23, 2010. In the fall 2011 Regulatory Agenda, EPA classified this rulemaking as a "Long Term Action Rule," indicating that rulemaking is not imminent.[137] Another entry in the same Regulatory Agenda indicates that EPA plans to explore regulatory and non-regulatory options for "clarifying the active and inert ingredient listing" of pesticide ingredients. That latter action is in the "Proposed Rule" stage. EPA anticipated issuance of a notice of proposed rulemaking in February 2012.[138] If EPA does commence rulemaking, and a proposed rule is published in the *Federal Register,* the rule will be scrutinized in accord with various executive orders concerning regulatory review of significant rules, and a regulatory analysis of costs and benefits will be submitted to the regulatory docket. Public comments may be submitted to the docket at that time.

Issues

Pesticide manufacturers often claim the identities of inert ingredients to be proprietary, and disclose them only to EPA and its contractors under a "confidential business information" agreement. Sometimes even the registrants of pesticide formulations are not told the identities of proprietary ingredients or mixtures supplied by manufacturers. EPA and the petitioners believe that registrants and consumers should be able to ascertain whether the products they use contain potentially hazardous ingredients. With such information, many believe the market should operate more efficiently by allowing formulators and consumers to choose products that include or exclude such ingredients rather than relying on government regulators to determine what ingredients are safe. EPA has announced that it is committed to improving public availability of such information to assist consumers and users of pesticides in making informed decisions and to reduce the presence of potentially hazardous ingredients in pesticides. After EPA required disclosure of 50 inert ingredients in 1987, most of them were removed from pesticide products.[139] On the other hand, pesticide manufacturers might object to disclosure if it would reveal information deemed to be proprietary, lead to loss of sales, or jeopardize market advantage relative to competitors. This issue could be of interest to the agriculture community given the use of pesticide products by producers.

CRS Contact

Linda-Jo Schierow, Specialist in Environmental Policy, 7-7279, lschierow@crs.loc.gov.

---

[135] U.S. Environmental Protection Agency, 52 *Federal Register* 13305, April 22, 1987.

[136] U.S. Environmental Protection Agency, "Public Availability of Identities of Inert Ingredients in Pesticides," 74 *Federal Register* 68215-68223, December 23, 2009.

[137] EPA, Unified Regulatory Agenda, Fall 2011, January 20, 2012, p. 262, RIN: 2070-AJ62, http://www.regulations.gov/#!documentDetail;D=EPA-HQ-OA-2012-0077-0001.

[138] Ibid., p. 243, RIN: 2070-AJ79.

[139] U.S. Environmental Protection Agency, "Public Availability of Identities of Inert Ingredients in Pesticides," 74 *Federal Register* 68217, December 23, 2009.

Clean Water Act Permits for Pesticide Application

For the more than 30 years since Congress enacted the Clean Water Act (CWA) and the Federal Insecticide, Fungicide, and Rodenticide Act (FIFRA), little apparent direct conflict existed between the two laws. EPA's operating principle during that time was that pesticides used according to the requirements of FIFRA do not require regulatory consideration under the CWA. EPA had never required CWA permits for use of FIFRA-approved materials, and EPA rules did not specifically address the issue.[140]

Recently, however, EPA's interpretation and operating practice were challenged in several court cases. At issue has been how FIFRA-approved pesticides that are sprayed over or into waters are regulated and, specifically, whether the FIFRA regulatory regime is sufficient alone to ensure protection of water quality or whether such pesticide application requires approval under a CWA permit. The issue arose initially over challenges to some routine practices in the West (weed control in irrigation ditches and spraying for silvicultural pest control on U.S. Forest Service lands). It drew more attention in connection with efforts by public health officials to combat mosquito-borne illnesses such as West Nile virus. The litigation created uncertainty over whether application of pesticides and herbicides to waterbodies requires a CWA water discharge permit.

Status

EPA tried to promulgate policy to clarify the relationship of the two laws and to address conflicts resulting from several judicial rulings, ultimately in a regulation issued in 2006 that attempted to specify circumstances in which pesticides applied to U.S. waters do not require CWA permits. That rule was challenged by multiple parties, and in January 2009, a federal appellate court vacated the rule.[141] As a result, persons who spray pesticides on or near water are now required to obtain a CWA permit.

The federal court's ruling appeared to leave little room for EPA to fashion a new rule consistent with the agency's long-standing view that FIFRA-compliant applications do not require CWA permits. Industry groups subsequently petitioned the Supreme Court to review the case, but the Court denied the petition.

To meet the court's mandate, EPA issued a pesticide general permit, or PGP, on October 31, 2011.[142] General permits cover categories of point sources that have common elements and that discharge the same types of wastes. Generally, permits allow the permitting authority to allocate resources efficiently, especially when there are a potentially large number of permittees, and to provide timely permit coverage. EPA estimates that the universe of affected activities that for the first time will be subject to CWA permits is approximately 5.6 million applications annually, which are performed by 365,000 applicators covering four use patterns: (1) mosquito and other flying insect pest control; (2) aquatic weed and algae control; (3) aquatic nuisance animal control;

---

[140] For more information on pesticide use and water quality, see CRS Report RL32884, *Pesticide Use and Water Quality Are the Laws Complementary or in Conflict?*.

[141] *National Cotton Council of America v. U.S. Environmental Protection Agency*, 553 F.3d 927 (6th Cir. 2009).

[142] U.S. Environmental Protection Agency, "Final National Pollutant Discharge Elimination System (NPDES) Pesticide General Permit for Point Source Discharges From the Application of Pesticides; Notice of final permit," 76 *Federal Register* 68750-68756, November 7, 2011.

---

and (4) forest canopy pest control. The permit covers about 500 different pesticide active ingredients that are contained in approximately 3,700 product labels.

The permit applies to a variety of entities, including agricultural interests involved in crop and timber tract production, forest nurseries, and operating irrigation systems; pesticide and agricultural chemical manufacturing; mosquito or other vector control districts and commercial applicators that service them; utilities (e.g., electric power, natural gas, water supply and wastewater); and government agencies and departments engaged in air and water resource management and conservation. It requires all operators to minimize pesticide discharges to waters by practices such as using the lowest effective amount of pesticide product that is optimal for controlling the target pest. It also requires operators to prepare pesticide discharge management plans to document their pest management practices. Permittees must monitor for observable adverse effects in the treatment area and where the pesticides are discharged to U.S. waters. The permit does not cover agricultural stormwater runoff or irrigation return flow, as these discharges are statutorily exempt from CWA permitting, and it also does not cover terrestrial application to control pests on agricultural crops or forest floors. Thus, because pesticide applications to land that do not result in point source discharges of pesticides to U.S. waters do not require permit coverage, EPA says that many farms are not affected by the court's decision and do not need CWA permits. The EPA general permit will apply in states and areas where EPA is the NPDES permitting authority, but it is expected to be a model for other states to develop their own general permits.[143] General permits issued by the other states must meet CWA guidelines and also may be more stringent than EPA's requirements.

Most entities subject to the EPA general permit were automatically covered, while some pesticide applicators with more significant discharges must submit a notice of intent (NOI) to be covered by the PGP. For example, any federal or state agency that conducts pest management as an integral part of its operation, and special-purpose districts with a specific responsibility to control pests, must submit a NOI. The permit took effect in January 2012, but EPA delayed enforcing its requirements until March 1, in order to focus on outreach and compliance assistance.

In an effort to halt EPA's regulatory activity, in March 2011, the House passed legislation (H.R. 872) that is intended to overturn the court's 2009 ruling by exempting aerial pesticide application activities from clean water permit requirements. The Senate Committee on Agriculture, Nutrition and Forestry approved the bill without amendment in June 2011.

Issues

General permits cover categories of point sources that have common elements and that discharge the same types of wastes. They allow the permitting authority to allocate resources efficiently, especially when there is a large number of potential permittees. Permitting procedures are streamlined and simplified, compared with CWA individual permits. Still, many agricultural industry groups are fearful that the court's ruling and EPA's general permit will lead to more burdensome and potentially costly requirements.

---

[143] The CWA authorizes EPA to delegate NPDES permitting authority to qualified states, and EPA has done so for the majority of states. For this permit, EPA will be the permitting authority in Massachusetts, New Mexico, Oklahoma, Alaska, Idaho, and the District of Columbia and for certain tribal lands.

CRS Contact

Claudia Copeland, Specialist in Resources and Environmental Policy, 7-7227, ccopeland@crs.loc.gov.

Pesticide Drift Labeling

State agencies and EPA receive numerous complaints every year claiming harm (or risk) to beneficial insects or to human health from exposure to pesticides that have drifted beyond the fields targeted for application. Current federal and state regulations aim to protect agricultural workers and non-target animals and plants, but opinions differ about the adequacy of such regulations. Drift issues were addressed in recent years by an EPA advisory committee of stakeholders, which recommended revisions to pesticide product labels to improve clarity and consistency, making the label instructions more comprehensible for applicators and facilitating enforcement by states. EPA issued proposed guidance in response to these recommendations.[144]

Pesticide drift is also the subject of a citizen petition received by EPA on October 13, 2009. Earthjustice, Farmworker Justice, and several other organizations requested that EPA assess exposure of children to pesticide drift and incorporate this information into risk assessments in support of registration decisions. They also requested interim prohibitions on the use of certain pesticides near homes, schools, and other places where children congregate.

Status

EPA issued the proposed labeling guidance and requested public comments on the citizen petition on November 4, 2009. The original periods for public comment on the labeling proposal and the petition were extended, but the comment periods ended March 5, 2010. EPA revised the guidance and will issue it in the form of a pesticide registration notice (e.g., PR Notice 2012-X).[145]

Issues

Some public health advocacy groups argue that the proposed label changes are "too little, too late." Nevertheless, bee-keepers and some state enforcement officials urge rapid adoption of the new policy. Thirty-eight congressional representatives signed a letter dated November 20, 2009, asking EPA to require no-spray buffer zones for drift-prone pesticides of at least 60 feet for ground applications and 300 feet for aerial applications from homes, schools, parks, day care centers, and other places where children may congregate.[146] But EPA appears to have decided against such prescriptions, opting instead for a "performance-based" approach based on a goal of preventing "harm."[147]

---

[144] EPA, Pesticide Spray and Dust Drift, December, 2009, http://www.epa.gov/pesticides/factsheets/spraydrift.htm.

[145] EPA, Drift Labeling PR Notice for the Pesticide Program Dialogue Committee, October 2011, Arlington, VA, November 14, 2011, http://www.epa.gov/pesticides/ppdc/2011/october/session2-spraydrift.pdf.

[146] Letter from Rep. Keith Ellison, Member of Congress, Rep. Raul Grijalva, and Rep. Donna Christensen, Member of Congress, et al. to Lisa Jackson, U.S. Environmental Protection Agency Administrator, EPA-HQ-OPP-2009-0628-0015, November 20, 2009, http://www.regulations.gov/#!documentDetail;D=EPA-HQ-OPP-2009-0628-0015.

[147] EPA, Drift Labeling PR Notice for the Pesticide Program Dialogue Committee, October 2011, Arlington, VA, November 14, 2011, http://www.epa.gov/pesticides/ppdc/2011/october/session2-spraydrift.pdf.

On the other hand, some producers, pesticide applicators, and agricultural groups argued that the proposed label language was too vague and would invite litigation. For more than a year, according to lawyers for pesticide producers,

> [EPA] has maintained its position that its policies will define unallowable drift to be that which "may cause" harm from the pesticide—which the users and registrants of pesticides believe to be an extreme (and not authorized) extension of the current FIFRA standard of "does not cause unreasonable risk." This distinction is more than semantics, since the criticism of EPA's position is that it would provide for a subjective standard placing [a] user of pesticide who followed every label instruction in jeopardy of a possible enforcement action even if "harm" has not occurred. The debate has been going on for years, and EPA has attempted to reassure critics that no new, more restrictive, standard is being imposed.[148]

The revised notice does not require label changes, but requires pesticide use in a manner that does not "harm" people or non-target organisms. The revised notice drops the language proposed in 2009 which would have prohibited pesticide use that "could cause an adverse effect."[149]

CRS Contact

Linda-Jo Schierow, Specialist in Environmental Policy, 7-7279, lschierow@crs.loc.gov.

Atrazine

Atrazine, a herbicide in use for at least 50 years, is one of the most widely used agricultural pesticides in the United States today.[150] It is used primarily on corn and sorghum in the Midwest. Atrazine is particularly useful for controlling broadleaf and grassy weeds in fields where no-till or low-till methods are employed to reduce topsoil erosion. These and other uses of atrazine are licensed by EPA, which registers pesticide active ingredients, as well as formulated products, for specified uses under specified conditions under the Federal Insecticide, Fungicide, and Rodenticide Act (FIFRA) and the Federal Food, Drug and Cosmetic Act (FFDCA). The latter law applies only to pesticides used on food and animal feed crops. For more information about pesticide laws, see CRS Report RL31921, *Pesticide Law: A Summary of the Statutes*. Recommended rates of application and other conditions of atrazine use are specified on the EPA-approved labels of various formulated pesticide products. It is illegal to use any pesticide product in a manner inconsistent with label instructions.

Widespread and relatively heavy use of atrazine, its persistence in the environment, reports of atrazine contamination of surface and drinking water,[151] and scientific studies indicating that exposure to atrazine might disrupt the normal action of hormones in animals[152] have prompted

---

[148] Bergeson & Campbell, Commentary, "2011 Predictions for EPA's Office of Chemical Safety and Pollution Prevention," January 3, 2011, http://www.lawbc.com/news/docs/2011/01/010311-fedreg.htm.

[149] EPA, Drift Labeling PR Notice for the Pesticide Program Dialogue Committee, October 2011, Arlington, VA, November 14, 2011, http://www.epa.gov/pesticides/ppdc/2011/october/session2-spraydrift.pdf.

[150] Atrazine is the common name for 6-chloro-N2-ethyl-N4-isopropyl-1,3,5-triazine-2,4diamine.

[151] Jack E. Barbash, Gail P. Thelin, Dana W. Kolpin, and Robert J. Gilliom, Distribution of Major Herbicides in Ground Water of the United States, U.S. Geological Survey, Water-Resources Investigations Report 98-4245 Sacramento, California, 1999, http://water.usgs.gov/nawqa/pnsp/pubs/wrir984245/wrir984245.pdf.

[152] U.S. Geological Survey, "Commonly Used Herbicide Adversely Affects Fish Reproduction," USGS Newsroom, http://www.usgs.gov/newsroom/article.asp?ID=2467&from=news_side.

EPA's pesticide office to review atrazine registration more frequently than it has reviewed most other pesticide registrations. Scrutiny of atrazine began at least 20 years ago, and has continued, as new scientific hypotheses and studies have developed. For example, in November 1994, EPA initiated a "Special Review" of the potential risks posed by atrazine and related triazine pesticides to agricultural workers and to drinking water consumers.[153] This review is ongoing. EPA issued a re-registration eligibility decision (RED) for atrazine April 6, 2006.[154]

In recent years, many scientific studies have been published indicating possible risks posed by atrazine to animals, as well as to human health. In addition, new monitoring data collected in the Midwest by Syngenta, a major manufacturer of atrazine, recently became available for analysis. In response, EPA announced October 7, 2009,[155] that it would again re-evaluate atrazine research. On the basis of its review, EPA will decide whether further regulatory restrictions are necessary to prevent unreasonable effects on human health or the environment. EPA called for the assistance of its FIFRA Scientific Advisory Panel (SAP) to review the agency's plans for evaluating human epidemiological studies as well as studies of laboratory animals and wildlife.

Status

On November 3, 2009, EPA presented its plan for the atrazine reevaluation to the SAP.[156] In 2010, the agency held three SAP meetings to address atrazine issues. In summer 2011, another peer review was conducted concerning the findings of the Agricultural Health Study, a large epidemiological study of agricultural workers and their families. That study is evaluating the potential association between human atrazine exposure and cancer risk.[157] According to EPA, "[t]he SAP's recommendations will help EPA determine the appropriate next steps in the Special Review regarding cancer and drinking water issues."[158] The conclusions of the SAP, which were posted to the regulatory docket on October 31, 2011, also might influence EPA's risk assessment of atrazine and subsequent reregistration decisions.[159] Additional documents related to the evaluation of atrazine are in the regulatory docket.[160]

---

[153] Richard P. Keigwin, Jr., Director, EPA Pesticide Re-evaluation Division, EPA response to Szmuszkovicz letter regarding the special review status of EPA's current Atrazine review, August 13, 2010, http://www.regulations.gov/#!documentDetail;D=EPA-HQ-OPP-2003-0367-0191.

[154] EPA, Decision Documents for Atrazine, April 6, 2006, http://www.epa.gov/oppsrrd1/REDs/atrazine_combined_docs.pdf.

[155] U.S. Environmental Protection Agency, "Atrazine Updates," current as of March 2011, http://www.epa.gov/oppsrrd1/reregistration/atrazine/atrazine_update.htm.

[156] EPA, U.S. Environmental Protection Agency Presentation of the Approach to Reevaluate Atrazine, November 3, 2009, http://www.epa.gov/scipoly/sap/meetings/2009/november/110309meetingtranscripts.pdf.

[157] For more information on the Agricultural Health Study, see http://www.aghealth.nci.nih.gov/.

[158] Richard P. Keigwin, Jr., Director, EPA Pesticide Re-evaluation Division, EPA response to Szmuszkovicz letter regarding the special review status of EPA's current Atrazine review, August 13, 2010, http://www.regulations.gov/#!documentDetail;D=EPA-HQ-OPP-2003-0367-0191.

[159] EPA, Re-Evaluation of Human Health Effects of Atrazine: Review of Non-Cancer Effects, Drinking Water Monitoring Frequency, and Cancer Epidemiology, Docket ID: EPA-HQ-OPP-2011-0399, November 14, 2011, http://www.regulations.gov/#!docketDetail;rpp=10;po=30;D=EPA-HQ-OPP-2011-0399.

[160] EPA, Re-Evaluation of Human Health Effects of Atrazine: Review of Non-Cancer Effects, Drinking Water Monitoring Frequency, and Cancer Epidemiology, Docket ID: EPA-HQ-OPP-2011-0399, November 14, 2011, http://www.regulations.gov/#!docketDetail;rpp=10;po=30;D=EPA-HQ-OPP-2011-0399.

Issues

Some policymakers and industry leaders are concerned about the continuing reviews of atrazine and similar herbicides. Chemical producers, distributors, and users are concerned that these reviews may lead to new restrictions or cancellation of pesticide uses. The potential cost to growers and consumers if EPA would cancel or restrict registration for atrazine could be considerable. On the other hand, public health advocates, some consumers of drinking water, and advocates for environmental protection have argued that new restrictions on atrazine uses should be considered and may be warranted if current regulations do not ensure with a reasonable certainty that atrazine use on food will pose no harm to human health and that atrazine use in general will not pose an unreasonable risk to the environment.

CRS Contact

Linda-Jo Schierow, Specialist in Environmental Policy, 7-7279, lschierow@crs.loc.gov.

Endangered Species Act (ESA)

The Endangered Species Act (ESA)[161] protects species identified as endangered or threatened with extinction and attempts to protect the habitat on which they depend. It is administered primarily by the Fish and Wildlife Service (FWS), and by the National Marine Fisheries Service (NMFS) for certain marine and anadromous species. Dwindling species are listed as either endangered or threatened according to assessments of the risk of their extinction. Once a species is listed, legal tools are available to aid its recovery and to protect its habitat. The ESA can become the visible focal point for underlying situations involving the allocation of scarce or diminishing lands or resources, especially in instances where societal values may be changing, such as for the forests of the Pacific Northwest, the waters of the Klamath River Basin, or the polar environment.

Status

In the case of agriculture, actions of some federal agencies may affect a very wide area or a region and have the potential to affect many listed species. Perhaps the most widely known of such agency actions is the registration and use of pesticides, such as those described in the "Pesticide Drift Labeling" section, above. EPA is required to consult with either FWS or NMFS on whether the use of a pesticide might jeopardize the continued existence of a listed species or adversely modify critical habitat. To mitigate harm, EPA might need to include on a label restrictions on use (such as total area, weather conditions, distance from a particular habitat type, etc.). Consultation, or lack of consultation, between agencies in such cases has sometimes been contentious and has led to citizen lawsuits to enforce the ESA. On several occasions, EPA has been sued for failing to comply with ESA requirements on some of its pesticide regulation decisions.[162]

---

[161] Act of December 28, 1973, P.L. 93-205, 87 Stat. 884. 16 U.S.C. §§1531-1544. For a more detailed discussion of ESA and its structure, see CRS Report RL31654, *The Endangered Species Act A Primer*.

[162] See *Washington Toxics Coalition v. EPA*, 413 F.3d 1024 (9th Cir. 2005) and *Center for Biological Diversity v. EPA*, 2010 wl 2143658 (N.D. Cal. May 17, 2010). For more on the temporary change and issues surrounding its issuance and withdrawal, see CRS Report RL34641, *Changes to the Consultation Regulations of the Endangered Species Act (ESA)*. (continued...)

Issues

For activities on privately owned land such as farms and ranches, the primary direct impact of the ESA is through the law's prohibitions on taking of listed species. The word *take* means "to harass, harm, pursue, hunt, shoot, wound, kill, trap, capture, or collect, or to attempt to engage in any such conduct."[163] Thus, such activities as applying pesticides to kill insects eaten frequently by an endangered bat species, or cutting down a tree that contains the nestlings of an endangered bird, would constitute a taking. Plants have substantially less protection under the ESA, so removing an endangered plant on private land would trigger an ESA violation only under extremely limited circumstances.[164]

If federal actions (or actions of non-federal parties that require a federal approval, permit, or funding) might adversely affect a listed species as determined by FWS (or NMFS, depending on the species), the federal action agencies must complete a biological assessment.[165] The assessment is used to determine whether formal consultation is necessary.[166] Through consultation with either FWS or NMFS, federal agencies must ensure, based on "the best scientific and commercial data available," that their actions are "not likely to jeopardize the continued existence" of any endangered or threatened species, nor to adversely modify critical habitat.[167] This is referred to as a Section 7 consultation. "Action" includes any activity authorized, funded, or carried out by a federal agency, including permits and licenses.

CRS Contact

Lynne Corn, Specialist in Natural Resources Policy, 7-7267, lcorn@crs.loc.gov, or Linda-Jo Schierow, Specialist in Environmental Policy, 7-7279, lschierow@crs.loc.gov.

(...continued)

[163] 16 U.S.C. §1532. Harassment and harm are further defined by regulation at 50 C.F.R. §17.3.

[164] See 16 U.S.C §1538(a)(2).

[165] 16 U.S.C. §1536(c).

[166] 50 C.F.R. §402.12(a). Informal consultations are also important, and may be as simple as a federal official of one agency calling an FWS or NMFS official to describe a small project and to find out whether there are any listed species in the vicinity.

[167] 16 U.S.C. §1536(a).

Author Contact Information

Megan Stubbs, Coordinator
Analyst in Agricultural Conservation and Natural
Resources Policy
mstubbs@crs.loc.gov, 7-8707

Claudia Copeland
Specialist in Resources and Environmental Policy
ccopeland@crs.loc.gov, 7-7227

M. Lynne Corn
Specialist in Natural Resources Policy
lcorn@crs.loc.gov, 7-7267

Robert Esworthy
Specialist in Environmental Policy
resworthy@crs.loc.gov, 7-7236

James E. McCarthy
Specialist in Environmental Policy
jmccarthy@crs.loc.gov, 7-7225

Jonathan L. Ramseur
Specialist in Environmental Policy
jramseur@crs.loc.gov, 7-7919

Linda-Jo Schierow
Specialist in Environmental Policy
lschierow@crs.loc.gov, 7-7279

Brent D. Yacobucci
Section Research Manager
byacobucci@crs.loc.gov, 7-9662

Randy Schnepf
Specialist in Agricultural Policy
rschnepf@crs.loc.gov, 7-4277